A VACATION WITH THE LORD

A VACATION WITH THE LORD

A PERSONAL, DIRECTED RETREAT WITH

THOMAS H. GREEN, S.J.

AVE MARIA PRESS
Notre Dame, Indiana 46556

Imprimi Potest:
   Rev. Bienvenido Nebres, S.J.
   March 21, 1986
Nihil Obstat:
   Rev. Leo Vandromme, C.I.C.M.
Imprimatur:
   Jaime L. Cardinal Sin
   February 21, 1986

Library of Congress Catalog Card Number: 86-71143
International Standard Book Number: 0-87793-342-1
                                    0-87793-343-X (pbk.)
Printed and bound in the United States of America.

CONTENTS

INTRODUCTION

This book, intended as a companion or guide for an eight-day retreat based on St. Ignatius Loyola's *Spiritual Exercises*, originated as a cassette series of four 90-minutes tapes, also entitled *A Vacation With the Lord* (Ave Maria Press, 1985). Each side of 45 minutes provided guidelines for prayer for one of the eight days. To my joy, the cassettes were well received. Many listeners, including several who had never before had the opportunity to make a personalized retreat, wrote to tell me they had used them for their own retreats. Some suggested, however, that it would be more helpful and less expensive to have the matter in book form. When I presented the suggestion to Frank Cunningham, my editor, he and the staff of Ave Maria Press agreed. In fact, they arranged to have the tapes transcribed and provided me with a copy of the transcription.

When I began to edit the typescript for book publication, I discovered that there is a great difference between the two media: voice and print. I wished to retain the conversational, personal, unfootnoted style of the cassettes. But it was necessary in print to have paragraph divisions and complete sentences. Moreover, the colloquial and occasionally circuitous style of the cassettes (or of a lecture) was not fully transferable to the printed page. What follows, then, is the fruit of three months of editorial revision. The content is essentially the same, although several points have been amplified or clarified. As far as possible, the tone and style of the cassettes have been preserved. It is still my hope that the reader will feel that I am speaking to her or to him personally, and the purpose of our "conversation" is not merely to inform but to inspire, to move to prayer.

The primary purpose of *A Vacation With the Lord* in both its incarnations is to enable sincere pray-ers to discover (or to rediscover) the riches of St. Ignatius' *Spiritual Exercises* after many decades of obscurity and misunderstanding. Ample scholarly and professional work has been done on the *Exercises* in recent times by Jesuits such as Hugo Rahner, William Peters and David Stanley, as well as by centers of spirituality such as that in Guelph, Ontario, Canada. In this sense, we have been abundantly blessed. Yet, at the "grassroots" level of actual retreat-making, many people still find the *Spiritual Exercises* a closed book. Or if it is "open," it is seen as mechanical and restrictively methodological, alien to the spirit of spontaneity and flexibility which characterizes most good writing on prayer today.

The difficulties people found with the *Exercises* as interpreted and presented for many years were real, and the objections raised were often well-taken. But, as I discuss briefly in day one, I believe these problems and flaws are not due to Ignatius and the *Exercises*. He, too, would have many objections to retreat practices of the recent past. As mentioned below, this can be explained in part by the extraordinary growth of the retreat movement over the 450 years since Ignatius wrote his little book. No doubt another significant factor has been the strong moralistic and anti-contemplative bent of most 19th and early 20th-century spirituality. It is likely, as several of my Protestant friends have suggested to me, that we Catholic pray-ers were much more "Protestantized" than we ever suspected or even thought possible.

While we can leave it to competent historians to analyze the reason for this deviation from the original Ignatian (and Catholic) spirit in retreats and in prayer in general, it will help to summarize here the contrast of which I am speaking. This will be spelled out in all the pages to follow, but it can be epitomized in the title of this book: *A Vacation With the Lord.* Whatever retreats of the past may have been, very few retreatants would have characterized their experience as a "vacation." Indeed many even among truly committed and generous priests and religious still face the prospect of their annual retreat with apprehension. They see it as a time of "soul-scraping," an uncomfortable confrontation with the demands of God and with their own inadequacy and infidelity. We could even say, in terms that will be clearer when we present days two and three below, that their whole idea of a retreat begins and ends with the first week of the *Spiritual Exercises.*

By contrast, my own experience has been that the annual retreat is truly the best time of the year, and this despite the fact that as far as I can judge many of the fearful retreatants described above are deeper and more generous than I am. As my own exposure to giving retreats broadened, it seemed that many others were confirming my own experience: Once the *Spiritual Exercises* were taken on their own terms and not according to the preconceived expectations of past decades, they were the means to a truly joyous and liberating encounter with a loving God. They do demand a radical honesty, a willingness to stand naked before the Lord. But "the truth will set you free," especially when that truth is approached and confronted in a psychologically sound and authentically Christian way. When, as Father William Connolly, S.J., has said so well, we focus on strength rather than on weakness. Judging from all my personal experience as a pray-er and as a retreat director, this is the Lord's own way of dealing with us. It is clearly the way of St. Ignatius in the *Spiritual Exercises.*

This book is an attempt to share that experience with an even wider audience. It can be used by retreat directors as a supplement to their own personal one-to-one direction of their retreatants; by retreatants who make a retreat with a director, the book providing the content input (together with the references to the *Spiritual Exercises* and to the scriptures given for each day) while the director provides the personal co-discernment; and by mature retreatants who wish to be "alone with the Lord." In my judgment the last situation is the ideal or the goal, since the role of a good director is not to make directees dependent but to free them for the Lord. After several directed retreats, a mature retreatant should be able to go off by himself or herself to encounter the Lord, provided that a good director is available for consultation if doubts or difficulties arise.

In addition, the book can be used (as the text actually envisions) for a "closed" retreat of eight or 12 days. But it could also be used for a "retreat in daily life," the situation St. Ignatius describes in number 19 of the *Exercises* where a pray-er of good will simply cannot get free for a closed retreat. Such a person (for example, the mother of a young family) could devote an hour each day to the *Spiritual Exercises,* spending several days on each of the daily themes given and prolonging the retreat over several weeks or months. Other adaptations are also possible. One sister friend, for example, told me that she has planned her monthly recollections for the year by using one of the original cassette talks for each month. She found that this gives a unity and flow to her recollections which would otherwise be lacking.

In every case the goal of the *Spiritual Exercises* as presented here is that expressed by St. Ignatius in the very first paragraph: "...just as taking a walk, journeying on foot and running are bodily exercises, so we call spiritual exercises every way of preparing and disposing the soul to rid itself of all inordinate attachments, and, after their removal, of seeking and finding the will of God in the disposition of our life for the salvation of our souls." The means are many and various ("every way"), and Ignatius is the great apostle of flexibility, echoing St. Teresa of Avila's "Do whatever most moves you to love." What is crucial is the goal, the end: to be free from "inordinate attachments" in order to be free for God and his will. And even the freedom *from*, while essential, is subordinate to the freedom *for*, as recent philosophers have insisted.

In such an experience totally centered on encountering God, this book, like a good director, is only "John the Baptist." The principal actors are the Lord and the retreatant. Thus it is that the book, as the *Spiritual Exercises* itself, has to be lived and not merely read. Indeed, it is but one of the many instruments the Lord might use to mediate the encounter in love between himself and the pray-er. In my own growth as a retreat director there have been many such John the Baptists, beginning with Father John McMahon, S.J., and Father Vincent Ryan, S.J. John, who died not long ago, was my tertian-instructor who first encouraged me to pursue my desire for the retreat apostolate. To this end he sent me to Vinnie at Christ the King Retreat House in Syracuse, New York. It was a good apprenticeship and Vinnie, still very much alive today, knows how much I owe to him.

Other John the Baptists in my life and ministry include Segundiano Honorie and Marciano Radam. Ding typed this manuscript, as he has several others, while Mars, despite what I say in day two, has kept alive for me many things more important than plants. My best mentors, though, have been those (numbering in the thousands by now) who have paid me the supreme compliment of entrusting themselves to my direction in retreats over the past 20 years. As is always true where the Lord is involved, I have received much more than I have given. May this book be a small token of my gratitude to them, as well as to Vinnie Ryan and John McMahon — and to the Lord, for taking the risk of placing in my weak hands this holiest and most fulfilling of all ministries.

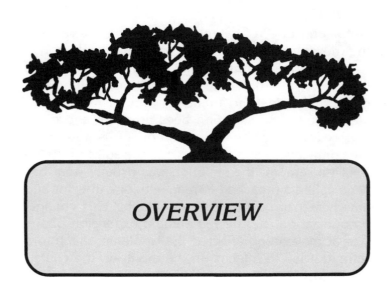

OVERVIEW

The Idea of a Retreat   The retreat movement in the church now has a history of about 450
years. It came into existence with the *Spiritual Exercises* of St. Ignatius Loyola at the beginning of the
age of the active religious communities. Prior to that
time, religious were either monks or lived in semi-
monastic religious communities such as the mendi-
cant Franciscans and Dominicans. In a certain sense,
in the monastic life one is "on retreat" all the time.
But with the advent of the strictly apostolic communities, St. Ignatius Loyola realized by the grace of
God and the inspiration of the Holy Spirit that there
was a great need for active apostles to "come aside
and rest awhile," as Jesus instructed his disciples to
do at certain important times in their lives.

Because of this need, the retreat movement began originally as a one-to-one experience — one di-

rector and one retreatant. But as time passed and the movement became more popular, people began to make retreats annually, not just once or twice in a lifetime. When the church's legislation required religious and priests to make an annual retreat, the ideal one-to-one situation became more and more impractical. Thus by the time most of us were making contact with and entering into the spirit of the retreat movement, the situation was usually what has been called a preached retreat, with one director and anywhere from 30 to 200 retreatants. This change, brought about by the remarkable expansion of the retreat movement, affected the whole approach to a retreat. It led to a focus on the input, on the conferences which the retreat director could give. It also led to a certain depersonalization: Since the director had to give one talk for many people, it was very difficult to meet them individually and to take account of each one's personal needs. The focus was thus more on the content presented than, as it should have been, on the interpretation of the individual's prayer experience which a good director could provide. The director became a lecturer rather than a co-discerner, and the retreatant was left to face the Lord (and the evil spirit) alone.

As we have been rediscovering lately, this was very far from what St. Ignatius intended, and very far, I believe, from what a real retreat should be. When the reaction to this group, content-centered approach set in around the time of Vatican II, the tendency was to shorten the retreat from eight days to six, or six to five, or four. The shortening was a result of dissatisfaction with the prepackaged, conference-type of retreat which then existed but, as more and more of us are coming to discover today, it was not really the solution. The problem with the old retreats was not their length; the problem was the style and the content. So in our day, by the grace of God, we have returned to the ideal of the one-to-one retreat, or one director with six or eight retreatants whom he or she can see individually each day.

In some situations we have what is called a semi-directed retreat, where one director can handle perhaps 18 or 20 retreatants. In such a case, the director gives one conference a day, presenting the general guidelines to the group for each of the days of the retreat, but still has time to see each of the retreatants at least on alternate days. This format can be quite helpful for more mature pray-ers, especially if they have had previous experience of an individually directed retreat. The input is taken care of in the conferences, and the individual adaptation, especially the personal discernment, is handled in the individual direction sessions.

As might be expected, and as has been the case, we face the problem that there simply are not enough qualified directors for everyone to make a directed or semi-directed retreat every year. This is especially true now that, again by the grace of God, more and more of the laity are realizing the value and the significance of a retreat for their lives. Thus, as the retreat movement recaptures something closer to its original form and ideal, we find ourselves confronted with a problem. Once people have made a directed or semi-directed retreat, it is very difficult for them in future years to go back to the preached retreat. So the question arises, for my directees and I am sure for many others: Once I have the good experience of a one-to-one, personalized retreat, where the focus is on personal experience and discernment rather than on content input, how do I proceed thereafter? It was to answer that question and meet that need that it occurred to me to do the cassette series from which this book originated. That is, I think it is possible once one has made one or two or a few good directed or semi-directed retreats to go more on one's own. The solution is not to go back to a preached retreat; at the same time we cannot expect to find an individual director every year, given our problems of personnel and charism. There should be another alternative.

A few years ago I drew up what I called an outline for a private retreat. (See pages 173-175.) The idea was that those who had acquired some sensitivity to the working of the Spirit could go off with this guideline, this outline, and make a retreat by themselves. If the goal of good direction, as I have stressed in my books, is precisely to free the directees — to bring them to the point where they can be discerning persons themselves — then it should be possible in some sense for people as they mature to make a retreat on their own.

All of the above presupposes a particular understanding of what a retreat really is. I see it not as a collection of reflections on isolated topics (for example the vows, social concern, the paschal mystery) nor as a super-examination of conscience or a time of soul-scraping, but as the title of this book indicates, a *vacation with the Lord.* That, I believe, is the leitmotif of my whole understanding of the retreat. It should be not the hardest time of the year, but the best time. There may be difficulties — almost surely there will be, since the retreat is a microcosm of life — but they should be the difficulties involved in doing something that we find immensely rewarding, that we look forward to as the deepest and richest time of the year.

If it is a vacation with the Lord, then I need to be relaxed. I always stress in my own retreats that if there is any tension, it probably will not be coming from the Lord, and I hope it won't be coming from me as the director. To remove any tension coming from the retreatant, I always suggest that three guidelines for a good retreat are, as a Dominican sister-friend of mine once noted, ESP: to *eat* well, to *sleep* well, and to *pray* the rest of the time. This means that I make it a real vacation. I don't just give the Lord part of my time and part of myself; rather I seek, in the classic monastic phrase, to *vacare Deo,* to be totally free for the Lord.

He is the host, and therefore this vacation has an element of uncertainty about it. I don't know whether he has planned a mountain-climbing vacation, a sleeping vacation, or a swimming vacation. I am a guest in his house; he is the one who plans the vacation. Thus there is naturally an element of uncertainty and perhaps even of anxiety, since I am not in control. This is especially true for us active apostles, who are by nature "control" people. Usually we are activists — that is what has brought us into the apostolic life, whether as religious or as lay persons. During these days we must try to really relax and let the Lord be the host.

Each of the chapters to follow will suggest the theme and the procedure for one day in an eight-day retreat. The whole could be adapted to a longer or a shorter time. In any case, we will try to follow the basic themes of the 30-day *Spiritual Exercises*. At the same time, I will suggest how we can bring them to the level of personal experience and personal commitment, as St. Ignatius Loyola clearly desired that we do.

The Tools of a Good Retreat   The "tools" that I would suggest for such a retreat are, first of all, some books. The most important, of course, is a good Bible; that is, one that I feel comfortable with, one that I can read easily, one that speaks not only to my head but to my heart. Personally, I find the *Good News Bible* readable and helpful. *The Jerusalem Bible* is also good, and there may be others depending on one's personal taste. But a good Bible is the basic tool.

Secondly, we need a copy of the *Spiritual Exercises* of St. Ignatius Loyola. Although we may think of that as a peculiarly Jesuit tool, it really is the first fully worked out retreat in the church, and it is the gift of God, I think we could say, for which Ignatius was canonized. The *Spiritual Exercises* embody his charism, given not only for Jesuits but for the whole church, as several popes in the course of the last 450 years have reaffirmed. Thus the *Exercises* are for all Christians. Of course there can be many different styles of retreat. In my course on retreat-giving, I get students from different congregations and traditions, as well as lay people. I have even had students who are Protestant ministers. There is, indeed, room for personal and congregational adaptation of the re-treat format. But, as I hope to show, these *Spiritual Exercises* are not primarily a Jesuit method but a se-ries of guidelines for the retreatant and the director which would be applicable to any retreat, whether given (or made) by a Dominican or a Franciscan, a lay person or a diocesan priest, by anyone.

The copy of the *Exercises* which I usually use is the translation by Louis Puhl, S.J., but the references which I will give are to the paragraph numbers, which have now become the standard mode of refer-ence. So almost any of the commonly available translations of the *Spiritual Exercises* should be usa-ble in connection with the references given. To my knowledge, the only widely used one which does not have the paragraph numbering is that of Anthony Mottola. It is a good translation but, unfortunately, it would be necessary to search a bit in Mottola to find the parts to which I refer. In Puhl or Fleming or any other of the available translations, the paragraph numbers referred to will be the same.

Finally, in addition to the Bible and the *Spiritual Exercises*, other books could be used to stimulate re-flection, especially if one is a beginner or needs more by way of the traditional retreat conference. One which I have found especially helpful is Father David Stanley, S.J.'s *A Modern Scriptural Approach to the Spiritual Exercises* (St. Louis, Mo., Institute of Je-suit Sources, 1973). Also good are Father Karl Rahner, S.J.'s *Spiritual Exercises* (Herder and Herder, 1965), and — especially for the guidelines and the great Ignatian thematic meditations — Father John English, S.J.'s *Spiritual Freedom* (Guelph, Ontario, Loyola House, 1973). But one who has more experience in prayer and in making retreats may well find the Bible and the text of the *Exercises* (along with my brief explanation) quite sufficient.

The second important tool of a good retreat is a journal. Journal workshops and keeping a journal of our prayer are fairly common today. I myself find it a very valuable tool for discernment. The idea is just to sit down for a few minutes, perhaps after each period of prayer, and to jot down in the journal what has happened in prayer. I find it most helpful to write talking to the Lord, because if I write talking to the book or to myself, it tends to be very "heady" — focused on ideas and insights; whereas, as we shall stress, it is our *feelings* that we discern. I find when I write talking to the Lord, for example: "Lord, this hour was very difficult. I found myself distracted and restless, unable to center on you. But I tried to persevere, and in the last moment or two I felt your peace and your reassurance that the time was not wasted . . . " — as I say, when I do it talking to the Lord, the journal very naturally focuses on my feelings. He knows all my ideas and insights already. It is what I felt and experienced which is uniquely me and which comes into focus when I write to him.

I see three values of a good journal in a retreat. First of all, we all tend to be introspective, to be looking over our shoulder at ourselves when we are praying. We tend to ask, "Am I really praying?" or "Is this really God?" In other words, we turn away from the actual prayer experience in order to look at ourselves praying, and that is not good. The journal, I believe, can be a great help in avoiding that introspection. When I am tempted to ask whether I am praying, whether this is really God, I can say: "No. There will be a time for that question after the prayer when I sit down with the journal. It is better just to go ahead and pray as best I can and not be analyzing my prayer now."

The second value of the journal is this: If I have a director, or if I myself am attempting to see the unity of the whole retreat experience as I go along, the journal can help me not to lose sight of the forest because of the trees. A good retreat is like the weather; it changes suddenly and unpredictably, and when we have dark days we tend to forget that the sun ever shone. As St. John of the Cross says, referring especially to the dark night, "When there is consolation we feel it will last forever; and when there is desolation we believe God is gone forever." The journal can help us to see these individual ups and downs as parts of a total experience. For that reason also, I always suggest to retreatants that the last prayer period in each day be a repetition of the whole day, asking for the grace of unity. I suggest they not use some new scriptural passage, but rather reread their journal for the whole day or for the whole time of the retreat up to that moment, asking always to see the unity of the total experience. I believe that in a good retreat the Lord has just one "message" for us. It is an exciting adventure to discover gradually, with the help of the journal and the daily repetition, what that message is.

The journal's third value is realized when you come to speak to the director, to share what has been happening in your prayer. Usually it is not good, I think, to show the journal to the director. If we do we will be writing it for the director, whereas it should be between the retreatant and the Lord. We should not be writing with a view to impressing someone else. But it can be very helpful before meeting the director to read over the journal to see what you wish to share.

In connection with this, the third tool in a good retreat ideally is a director. Even if you are making a private retreat, I would recommend that you try to make it where someone is available to whom you can talk if and when necessary. Even if you are not seeing the director on a daily basis, at least you know that he or she is there, available to co-discern if needed. If you do have a director, what should you share? Basically, I recommend two things. First of all, an overview, a general description of what has been happening in your prayer since last you met. If your last meeting was one or two days ago, what has been your experience over those one or two days? The journal will be helpful here. As you read it over before meeting the director, you can recall the flow of your experience since the last meeting. This general overview does not have to be in great detail; in 10 or 15 minutes you can give the director a sense of the general pattern of what has been happening in your prayer.

The second thing to share with the director is any specific parts of your experience which you feel need clarification or confirmation. Perhaps you are not sure if you are really hearing the Lord's voice. Or perhaps you experienced desolation and are not sure if you handled it properly. So the two elements of your sharing are a general overview of the flow of the retreat and any specific points needing clarification or confirmation. As we said earlier, the director is primarily an interpreter, a co-discerner of your encounter with the Lord. To fulfill this role, he or she depends on your sharing of your experience.

Structuring the Day   Having mentioned these three tools of a good retreat, let us turn to consider the structure of the day. There are two possibilities to choose from: You can either think in terms of five periods of prayer, five hours in the day, and make a schedule for yourself; or you can simply spend the *whole* day with the Lord. Some people by temperament and training need structuring in order to be at peace. If so, that is fine. Indeed it may be necessary for beginning pray-ers to have this structure. But it is also possible, and I find it more helpful as we mature, to simply spend the day with the Lord: to eat well and sleep well, and then give the remaining time to him without worrying about hours or schedules. When he goes for coffee, I go; when he takes a rest, so do I. I simply try to adapt to *his* rhythm. For people who are more mature and whose prayer life is more mature, I think this second possibility is ideal because it frees us from our own planning and enables us to be more sensitive to the Lord's leading. The flexibility can be a great help to discerning love.

It might be good to mention that it is also possible to make the retreat in an adapted form. Many of us, especially those with family or business responsibilities, do not have the time or leisure to set aside eight whole days just for retreat. St. Ignatius anticipated this problem (in the 19th annotation of the

Spiritual Exercises) when he suggested that such a re-treatant could pray for an hour or an hour and a half each day and extend the whole retreat over several months. The director could be seen every week or every two weeks. For one who can really *vacare Deo* and be free from everything for those days, the closed retreat is certainly preferable because it is much easier to maintain the quiet prayer atmosphere once the mood of the retreat has been established. But the Lord can work his wonders within narrow confines, provided we are as generous with him as we can be.

There are two further points concerning the structure of the day. Where possible I like to have the eucharistic liturgy before supper, as a culmination of the whole day's prayer. The Eucharist is the climactic and central act of our lives. It is the true focus of our whole life of prayer. Thus it can be beautiful to place it at the end of the retreat day as a gathering together of all the threads of our experience on that day, a sacramentalizing of all that has happened. The second point is related: I also like to begin the theme of the new day in the evening. I find it symbolically and psychologically significant that the Jewish day began in the evening. By reading the chapter of this book appropriate to the following day after the Eucharist in the evening, we can then "sleep on" the new theme. It can be germinating during the night, and we will then find ourselves ready to enter into it fully in the morning.

The Dynamics of the "Spiritual Exercises"
It will be helpful to say a word here about the dynamics of the *Spiritual Exercises*, since they will be

our guide as we vacation with the Lord. The *Exercises* are divided into four weeks, as St. Ignatius explains in the fourth of the introductory observations or "annotations," as they are called. (These annotations are among the readings which I will suggest for the first day.) The four weeks of the retreat, Ignatius tells us, are not calendar weeks but thematic weeks. That is, they vary in length (from about 12 days for the second week in a 30-day retreat, to about 5 days each for the third and fourth weeks), but they represent a division or progression in terms of the major themes of a good retreat.

The first week, which we will present on day two, is a time of self-knowledge and self-opening to God. It has often been presented as a time of sorrow for sin, but I think it is more adequately characterized as a time of seeing myself as God sees me.

The second week, by contrast, is the time for putting on the Lord Jesus. Having honestly confronted myself, having become, as it were, naked before the Lord in the first week, I now seek to be clothed, filled with Christ. This second week is the heart of the retreat, the most important part, and is the longest of the four weeks. As we shall explain for day two, however, the first week is perhaps the most *crucial* in the sense that knowledge of God in Christ Jesus and knowledge of self go hand in hand. In terms of our metaphor of emptying and filling, the Lord can fill us in the second week only to the extent that we have been able to hollow out a space for him in the first week.

The third and fourth weeks, which treat of Calvary and the resurrection, are also an important time in the *Exercises*. As we shall explain in the final chapters, they are a time of confirmation — confirmation not in the sense of making sure of God's word to us, but in the sense of strengthening us to live this word as we return to daily life.

To review the main points we have made: A good retreat, I believe, is a vacation with the Lord. It should be a joyous time — a time of hard work, probably, but a work that you thoroughly enjoy. When retreatants tell me at the end of a good retreat that they have never worked harder and yet have never been more rested and relaxed, I feel we have succeeded. They have been strenuously involved in a pursuit that they love, and they have a great feeling of satisfaction because of that.

DAY ONE:
The Grace of a Good Beginning

Let us note that on this first day of our retreat we have not yet begun the first week. If we see the four weeks, which we have just discussed, as a deepening of our knowledge of the Lord and of ourselves, we could say that the focus there is on the present moment: on this week of the retreat, this day, this moment in my life. In contrast, this first day corresponds to what St. Ignatius calls the "Principle and Foundation." What we do on this first day before we focus on the Lord's call to us at the present moment in our lives, is to paint in the background, as it were. I am not a painter, but I have the impression that an artist doing a realistic painting sketches in the background before focusing on the central subject. If that is a correct description of the way artists work, it provides an apt metaphor for this first day of a retreat. Our present experience of God during the coming week has to be seen against the background of the whole history of our relationship with him.

The Prayer of the First Day   For a beginner in the spiritual life, St. Ignatius, in paragraph number 23 of the *Spiritual Exercises*, talks about the principle and foundation of all of our lives: that God alone, his glory and our salvation, is the *end* of our lives, and that everything else in life is but a *means* to that end. When people are just beginning to know the Lord and themselves, when they have not yet seen their lives clearly in terms of means and ends, this is the topic and the grace of the first day: to recognize in my life, and to affirm, his glory and my salvation for his glory as the only legitimate end or goal of my life, and everything else in life as subordinated to that end. As Ignatius says, all things have to be used or set aside insofar as they help or hinder me in respect to my goal.

Usually as retreatants mature they find the principle and foundation meditation rather dry and difficult to repeat fruitfully. As I reflected on this fact in the light of my own experience over the years, I concluded that the reason is because mature retreatants, mature pray-ers whether lay or religious, have already faced and accepted the means-end hierarchy to which Ignatius refers. Although they may fail in living by it, it is not new to them nor is it questioned. It can be reaffirmed, but it is rather difficult to spend a whole day doing so. For this reason I would suggest that for most mature retreatants the grace of the first day would be not so much the principle and foundation simply as it is given by Ignatius, but a reflection on and an experience of God's personal love for me.

In other words, the principle and foundation of my life has a history already. Whatever the Lord will

do in these days of retreat he has been working toward all through my life and especially since the day
when I accepted him as my central love and sole
end. Even though the overall pattern of my life may
not be at all clear to me, for him my whole history is
one. This present moment of retreat is just one sen-
tence, if you will, in the conversation which is my entire life with the Lord. Thus I think it can be fruitful
and very beautiful during the first day to review the
history of God's acts of love in my life. (Cf. the outline on page 173.) This is what I would suggest for
your prayer. Perhaps you can begin by reaffirming
the principle and foundation in paragraph number
23 of the *Spiritual Exercises*. But then let that take
flesh during the day by reviewing the history of your
relationship with the Lord, the relationship which
has been built on that essential foundation.

I always suggest to retreatants that in each day
of the retreat they focus on the grace which they
seek. Here on the first day that grace would be an
experiential knowledge of God's personal love for
me as that has been revealed in countless ways
throughout my life. (Cf. the outline on page 173.)
This is a helpful initial grace in several ways. Most
importantly, as I have said, it paints in the background of the painting so that the central figure, my
experience of God in this retreat, is properly contex-
tualized. In addition, this is a very fruitful way for retreatants to settle down, since they usually come to
retreat direct from a busy life. If you are very, very
tired as you begin, you may have to sleep much this
first day. That is also fine, if you need it — just pray
when you wake up! The theme of God's love is personal and autobiographical, and so fairly easy to en-

ter into. It is also quite relaxing as we seek to settle down. Even if you do sleep much, that is better than struggling with fatigue the whole week. After all, you have the whole week for the Lord.

As I say, focus each day on the grace sought, and for this first day that is the experiential knowledge of God's personal love for you, a love which is based upon the fact that he is the center and the only end of your life, that only he can love you in this way, that only he can make a total claim on your love. Centering thus on the grace you seek, I would suggest you use whatever readings or prayer exercises will help you to realize this grace. The scriptural passages, the excerpts from the *Spiritual Exercises*, and perhaps the "conference" readings from a book like Stanley's are but means to the grace you seek. So use as much or as little of these means as you find helpful for the end you have in view.

What readings would be helpful in realizing the grace of the first day? By way of background I would recommend reading over paragraphs 1 to 20 in the *Spiritual Exercises*, in which St. Ignatius gives some fundamental guidelines for both the retreatant and the director. Read them over quietly outside the time of prayer. If anything is unclear, check with a good director to get the necessary clarification. For the actual prayer itself, paragraphs 21 and 22 and especially the principle and foundation in paragraph 23 will be helpful.

Some scripture passages which could help you to this experience of God's personal love for you are Isaiah 43:1-7 and 49:15-16. Also Psalms 23, 27, 42 and 139. Psalms 103, 104 and 105, about the history of God's love for his people and for the individual Israelite and his role as the lord of creation, are also beautifully appropriate. In the New Testament, the prologue to the gospel of St. John (1:1-18) and Ephesians 3:17-19, could be helpful. Notice that these selections are a sort of smorgasbord. The idea is not to use all of them, but to select any one or more which might help to the grace you seek. Always keep the grace as the focal point. Throughout the whole of the retreat, use as many or as few of the readings as are needed to realize the grace of the day. In fact, for this first day simply recalling the blessing of God throughout your whole life from the very moment of your conception might be quite enough, without any reading even from scripture. Simply to recall all the gifts of God to you — family, faith, education, vocation, even failings and trials — might be more than sufficient to fill you with a deep personal experience of God's love for you.

Throughout the retreat the point is to focus your prayer on the grace that you seek. For today that grace is to *experience* (in the heart and not merely in the head) God's personal love for you. So use whatever means are helpful in realizing this grace: a review of your life, one or more of the scripture passages suggested, or other scripture passages or reflections which the Lord may suggest to you.

Beginning With Philip   As a final suggestion, I propose a brief initial reflection for this evening (assuming that you are beginning the retreat in the evening as we recommended). A beautiful passage with which to start is Acts 8:26-40, the story of Philip and the eunuch in Gaza. The eunuch from

Ethiopia in Africa is returning from his visit to the temple in Jerusalem. Philip goes down to Gaza, sent by the Lord, not knowing why he is in this desert place on the border between Israel and Egypt. It is a dangerous place, where brigands and robbers operated then as they do now. Philip has no idea why the Lord has brought him here. But when this eunuch, who was probably both black and wealthy (Philip being neither of these), came along he was told to approach this man whom he had never seen before without even knowing what he was supposed to speak to him about. Yet he goes without question. The Jewish eunuch is reading from one of the servant songs of Isaiah (53:7-8) concerning a mysterious "suffering servant" whom the Jewish people (like St. Peter) never identified with the expected conquering Messiah. When the eunuch asks him to whom the song refers, Philip recognizes his call to proclaim to this stranger the good news of Jesus. The eunuch is led to faith in the risen Lord, and Philip baptizes him in this isolated desert place. The encounter ends as suddenly and as mysteriously as it began. After baptizing the eunuch, and without knowing how his newfound faith will ever be nurtured in remote Ethiopia, Philip is taken up by the hair of his head and set back down in his own country. Without even questioning his mysterious journey, he immediately begins to preach the good news where his feet touch the ground. God sent him to Gaza, God took him away, and Philip in his simplicity has no questions.

I think this is a beautiful passage with which to begin a good retreat. It presents clearly the ideal disposition of a generous retreatant, that disposition of

Philip which Marcel calls *disponabilité*, total availability to God. In this first hour, as a help to this total receptivity or availability, try to surface all of your hopes and your fears as you begin this retreat. What am I hoping for during my vacation with the Lord? What am I afraid of? Let all your hopes and fears surface in the company of Philip and the eunuch. Then begin your journal by jotting all of them down. Tell the Lord your hopes. But tell him also that he is the boss. Whatever he desires will be best for you. And, in the same spirit, surrender to him all of your fears as you begin this retreat. Then you can turn in genuine peace and trust to seek in this first day to experience his personal love for you.

> I pray that Christ will make his home in your hearts through faith. I pray that you may have your roots and foundation in love, so that you, together with all God's people, may have the power to understand how broad and long, how high and deep, is Christ's love. Yes, may you come to know his love — although it can never be fully known — and so be completely filled with the very nature of God (Eph 3:17-19).

DAY TWO:

To Know Myself As I Am Known

The Grace of the First Day   As we continue our vacation with the Lord on our second of eight days, it might be good to recall first what we considered yesterday. We mentioned that on the first day of a good retreat we focus on what St. Ignatius calls (in number 23 of the *Spiritual Exercises*) the first principle and foundation. He says there that our only end is to praise, reverence and serve God our Lord and by this means to save our soul, and that everything else on the face of the earth is a means to this double end. In the light of that basic principle, he tells us that we should become indifferent to other things, indifferent in the sense that they don't seek to become ends in our life, or to compete with our sole end which is the glory of God and our own salvation. In other words, we must keep our hierarchy of means and ends clear.

In a real sense this is the goal of the whole retreat. We do not start with this disposition perfectly
realized, but we should already recognize it at least
in our heads as the goal that we accept, even if our
feelings and our will find it difficult to surrender fully
to this hierarchy of means and ends. I mentioned
that for beginners it is necessary to confront the
principle and foundation as St. Ignatius gives it and
to really recognize and acknowledge that this is the
goal of my life. As we mature, however, that foundation has already been laid. We have already affirmed
that this is the basic guiding insight of our lives, that
we are committed to it, and so we focus more on the
grace that was suggested: God's personal love for us.
We "paint in" the history of how we have lived this
principle and foundation in all the years since we
first came to know and accept the Lord personally,
and of how he has been faithful and true in his response to our efforts.

As we said, the first day's grace is important because it helps us to come to quiet before the Lord; it
helps us also to that disposition of openness and receptivity which is so important in a good retreat. It
disposes us to hear the Lord's personal word to us today. We suggested several scripture passages which
could be used to this end, and I emphasized that for
me the focal point in all the spiritual exercises of St.
Ignatius is the grace that we seek. Therefore, I suggested that you use whatever helps to this grace. It is
not so important how much or how little of scripture
we use. Indeed, those in the "dry well" who are experiencing the dark night in prayer might find that they
use little or nothing of the input. That is fine, as long
as the grace which we seek is realized.

Now, in connection with this centering on the grace sought, I would stress today that, although we move into the second day and I will be suggesting a new theme, it is very important, as St. Ignatius insists in his introductory instructions, that you move at your own pace. The test of whether to move on into the new day and new grace is whether the grace we were seeking yesterday was given. If it has been given, if you feel that the Lord has allowed you to experience his personal love, then perhaps you feel ready to move on. If it was very difficult to settle down yesterday, then you could stay longer on the grace of the first day. Stay with it as long as necessary, until you feel that the grace has been given.

It could even be that at a given moment in someone's life the particular grace of the first day could occupy them throughout the whole retreat. That might be what they most need now. Someone for whom God has never been experienced as loving, someone who has never been able to relate to him personally perhaps because of his or her own family experience might well spend several days or even the whole retreat on the first day's grace. That would be a fine retreat. It might even be the turning point of his or her life.

But let us assume for the sake of these conferences that the grace of the first day has been given and that you feel ready to move on in the retreat.

The First Week in Context   We begin today what St. Ignatius calls the first week, the first of four. It is in a sense the beginning of the *Spiritual Exercises* proper, the encounter with God and my true self at the present moment of my life. The four "weeks" of the *Exercises* represent a flow from self-knowledge to an apostolic knowledge of God in Christ Jesus, and finally to confirmation in one's commitment to live and share this experienced union with the Lord. The first "week," which we begin today, is focused on self-knowledge, self-emptying. In a 30-day retreat we would dedicate six to eight days to this crucial theme. Here, since we are thinking in terms of an eight-day retreat, we will devote approximately two days to seeing ourselves as God sees us.

An analogy which I use to explain the dynamic which St. Ignatius has in mind in the *Exercises* is the idea of a pot of dead flowers or a dead plant. Several years ago I decided that I needed something alive in my room besides myself. Since it was not possible to have a wife, the safest thing seemed to be to get some green plants and pots. A friend gave me planters that she had made, and when I hung the planters from the ceiling and put the potted plants in them, it added a very nice touch to the room.

All was well until I went to the States a few years ago to visit my family and to write a book. I asked my friend Mars Marciano, who has been working at San Jose Seminary from time immemorial, if he would water the plants while I was away for several months. He happily agreed. When I came home, though, I found that the plants were both very well watered and, some at least, dead! Perhaps he had forgotten and the watering had come too late for the survival of the plants. Anyway, whatever the reason, I was left with a lot of dead debris in those pots. The only solution to the problem was to empty out the dead matter and replant. There was no sense lamenting over what had been lost. But before I could put new life in the pots, I had to clear out the dead matter with which they were filled.

As I thought of that experience over the years, I came to see that it is a good analogy for the dynamics of the first and second weeks of the retreat as Ignatius envisions them. The first week is the time to empty out the pot, which is ourselves, of all the dead matter — to hollow out a space for new life for God. The second week is the time when we are filled with the new life of Christ. This filling is the heart of the *Spiritual Exercises*, and even in this short retreat we will spend three to four days on the second week.

It is the positive side of our faith, the resurrection part of the paschal mystery theme, which is very appealing to people today. I find, in fact, that my students in the course on giving retreats usually like to cut short the first week. The theme of self-knowledge and sin-consciousness and honest self-confrontation is one that they don't find very appealing. They would much rather move to the more positive theme of the love of Christ. Usually I have a bit of a struggle until they themselves give a retreat as part of the course. Only then do they come to realize the importance of the first week.

I would say that the second week is the most *important*, because it is the heart of the retreat. But in a real sense the first week, with its focus on self-knowledge and hollowing out a space for God to fill, is the most *crucial*. I say that because I believe that if the first week is done well then the rest of the retreat follows almost automatically. If, however, we gloss over the first week or don't honestly face ourselves in the mirror of God's revelation, then the whole rest of the retreat is on a very shaky foundation. To shift our metaphor back to the plants and the pots, God cannot fill us if we are filled with ourselves. All the devotion, all the beautiful insights from the life of Jesus, flow over us and wash away because they have no place to settle. They can't take root in us because we are already filled with ourselves.

Probably the same insight underlies the conviction that the most important day of the Cursillo is the fourth day, that is, the rest of our life. It is easy to have an emotional weekend conversion, but it is very difficult to make it lasting, to experience it as something that permanently changes us. Not everybody who enters the Cursillo has a space for God to fill. So even though there is great excitement on the surface, very little of that sense of God can penetrate down into the bones, can find a place to reside permanently within the person.

In the first week, therefore, we seek to hollow out a space that God can fill. More accurately, we seek to allow *him* to hollow it out, because it is his grace which can do this: create a space in us which he, then, in the second week, and for the rest of our lives can fill with himself. We seek to allow him to hold a mirror up to ourselves that our real situation may be revealed to us, and that we may be truly open to Christ's healing coming in the second week.

It is striking to notice that in the first week of the *Exercises*, which includes paragraph numbers 24 to 90, St. Ignatius first provides a discussion of matters that has given him the reputation of being rather mechanical and plodding. He talks about the daily particular examination of conscience and the general examination of conscience. He gives detailed procedures for making these and, finally, in paragraph number 44 the method for making a general confession. These matters, especially the way Ignatius describes them, can seem to be extraordinarily detailed and even deadening, but two important points have to be noted. First of all, it is only *after* all of this matter that Ignatius indicates in number 45 what he calls the first exercise of the first week. Therefore, we should recognize that all of these discussions of the examen, general confession, communion and so forth are preliminary to the first exercise of the first week.

Also, and perhaps more importantly, he tells us in paragraph number 18 that these are the matters that should be given to someone who, as he says, "wishes no further help than some instruction and the attainment of a certain degree of peace of soul." This 18th annotation or introductory observation describes a person who for Ignatius, I would say, is not really a retreatant. For it seems that the matter referred to in paragraphs 24 to 44 is intended for those not yet ready to encounter God in any depth. What I should do with them is try to focus on the basics, on what the Cenacle Sisters have called pre-evangelization. I try to dispose them so that sometime in the future they could really make a retreat.

The Dynamic of the First Week Exercises

The techniques of paragraphs 24 to 44 could also be useful for a serious retreatant, but the exercises of the first week proper begin in number 45. What St. Ignatius provides for this whole first week are only

five exercises, although he indicates at the end of
the first week that he expects the retreat director to
expand this basic skeleton.

The format of those five exercises for the first
week is very interesting and revealing. What Ignatius
gives us is, first of all, a meditation on the triple sin:
of the angels, of Adam and Eve, and of some hypo-
thetical soul who is in hell for just one mortal sin. He
asks the retreatant to reflect on these three cases of
grave sin. It might be difficult to see what the point
of this is. Especially with our present better exegesis
of Genesis we might have problems even entering
into the sin of Adam and Eve as St. Ignatius takes it.
Similarly, we might find the sin of the angels, as described, too speculative. And we could object to the
theological soundness of the idea of a soul being
condemned to hell for a single sin, a single slip-up in
an otherwise good life. But I think that would be to
miss the point.

I still believe that for beginners, whom Ignatius
had in mind here, the dynamics of these five exercises are very, very fruitful. Let us first note the content of the five meditations given. The first, as we
saw, focuses on these three sin situations. The second, the third and the fourth exercises all focus on
my own self, my own sin, about which we will say
more shortly. The fifth is a meditation on hell, which
Ignatius says can be supplemented with other contemplations, for example, on death or judgment or
purgatory.

From this description of the five meditations
suggested I think we can see clearly that the heart of
the first week is the focus on my own situation be-

fore God. Three of the five meditations center on my own personal sin, and those are the three central ones, the second, the third and the fourth. Thus it seems fairly obvious that in some way the first meditation on the triple sin is an introduction to the whole grace of self-knowledge which we seek. I think it is a very wise introduction psychologically.

I feel that what Ignatius is doing here is what Nathan did with King David after David had sinned with Bathsheba and had her husband Uriah killed (2 Sm 12:1-10). Nathan told a little story about a rich man who had large flocks. When a guest came, rather then using one of his own many lambs, he took the only lamb of a poor man and sacrificed it in order to feed his guest. David is very angry when he hears the story; he thinks it is an actual happening and he says in anger, "That man must pay for his crime. It is a terrible thing, when he himself is so wealthy, to steal from a poor man." Only when David is properly agitated does Nathan say, "That man is you. You have many wives, you have all the wealth of the kingdom, and yet you killed Uriah and took his wife. This poor man had only one wife and only one life. You sacrificed him for your own convenience, despite the fact that you have so much more than he."

I think Ignatius is doing something very similar in the first exercise of the first week. When we focus on the triple sin we see sin outside of ourselves as it were; we don't yet have to put our own name to what we are seeing. He brings us very shrewdly and very gracefully to face the reality of sin before confronting us and saying, as Nathan said to David, "That man is you." We first contemplate the reality of sin from the outside. From that point of view whatever problems we have with the extra-biblical traditions about the angels or with the exegesis of Genesis are quite secondary to what Ignatius had in mind. The real grace we are seeking is, as he would put it for beginners in the first week, sorrow for sin. My sin. If looking at it outside of me first helps me to face what is a very painful reality, if it is easier to look at it objectively and then gradually be brought to the confrontation with myself, that is fine. But the real point is what I see *in me*.

One further clarification is needed. St. Ignatius' first week is often spoken about as a contemplation or a series of meditations on sin and sorrow for sin. I myself have spoken more or less in that vein for the past few paragraphs. But I don't think it is entirely correct. The graces that he suggests (and you recall that I have stressed both yesterday and today that the grace we seek is the heart of the matter) do seem at first glance to focus on sorrow for sin. For example, in number 48: "Here it will be to ask for shame and confusion, because I see how many have been lost on account of a single mortal sin, and how many times I have deserved eternal damnation." He has similar comments in indicating the graces to be sought in subsequent meditations. Thus in number 55 we read: "Here it will be to ask for a glowing and intense sorrow and tears for my sins."

But I think we have to look a bit deeper. For example, as we come to the end of the first meditation in number 53, we are asked to imagine Christ present before us and to talk to him: "I shall also reflect upon myself and ask, 'What have I done for Christ?' And as I behold Christ in this plight, nailed to the cross, I shall ponder upon what presents itself to my mind." What presents itself might be sorrow, it might be commitment, or it might be gratitude. But I really think that to talk about the first week as a meditation on sorrow for sin without any qualification misses what is really the central purpose here.

Let me put it this way: I have felt over the years, my own 35 years of making retreats and my own 20 years of giving retreats to others, that as people mature very often that grace of sorrow which was easy and natural to them in the beginning of their interior lives becomes difficult to recapture. That has happened to me also. And it is precisely that experience of my own and of others which has forced me to rethink what is the real purpose of this first week. I think the basic grace to which Ignatius is leading us could be best expressed as the grace to see myself as God sees me.

Ignatius speaks primarily in terms of sorrow for sin, and I think this is appropriate since he envisioned the exercises originally as for beginners in the interior life. It was only later that the practice of repeating the spiritual exercises and eventually the annual retreat came in. I think Ignatius would be the first to insist, as the earliest extant Jesuit "Directory" of guidelines for the *Exercises* indicates, that as we repeat the exercises year after year they are going to have to be adapted. For the beginner for whom Ignatius first wrote the most natural fruit of seeing myself as God sees me would be sorrow, sorrow that I have lived forgetful of God, sorrow that even if I have been good by the world's standards, I have really been so shallow, and such a sinner in ways I never suspected in my complacency.

As we grow, however, I don't believe that it will always or even often be possible to repeat that experience. I don't think we really should. I think the Lord himself resists it. Once that sorrow is part of our lives, we move on from there to other things besides tears. I myself am doubtful about the legend that Peter wept all his life because of his denial of Jesus. He too had to move on to other things. Indeed, that initial sorrow was the springboard for the great love which came later. But I think Peter had better things to do than to spend his whole life grieving over the past. Similarly, I would take as the grace of this first week to see myself as God sees me. This "seeing," which is the desired fruit of the next two days, may engender sorrow, humility, gratitude or awe. But it will involve being opened to God in a new and deeper way.

Means to True Self-Knowledge   How can we seek that grace today? As indicated on the outline (page 173), I would suggest three possible scripture passages, as well as another alternative or perhaps complementary approach which is more autobiographical. First, the scripture passages: One is Job, chapters 38 to 42, another the first epistle of St. John, and the third Paul's letter to the Romans, chapters 1, 2, 5, 7 and 8. Each reading is about five chapters in length, so just one should suffice for the day's prayer. How would you choose among them? It might be that the Lord draws you to one of them. If so, let him make the choice.

If not, a reflection on your situation before God today might help you to choose. That is, if you are wrestling with God, if that is how you see your present situation before him, I would suggest you use those final chapters of Job, 38 to 42. In chapter 38, when God finally begins to speak after Job and his friends have been talking for 37 chapters, his rebuke of Job is, I think, a very loving one. The whole point of Job is missed if we simply conclude that Job was being castigated, that God was reducing him to silence for daring to question the divine ways. I believe the point is very different and more loving. The Lord is telling Job, "How foolish you are to think that I have abandoned you." Job had said earlier, "Since you have abandoned me, why don't you kill me and get it over with?" And Yahweh says to him, "Look around you at the stars in the heavens, at the sunrise, at how the mountain goat gives birth." (Apparently the Jewish people saw the mountain goat pregnant but never saw it deliver; it must have disappeared into the mountains.) So God is saying to Job, "If you don't understand all these things, what makes you think that you understand my ways with you? If I care for the universe in ways that you cannot comprehend, how can you conclude that I have abandoned you?" It is a very beautiful passage, truly overwhelming when seen in that light. So if you have been wrestling with God in your own life, I would suggest these chapters of Job.

If your situation before the Lord is peaceful but shallow, somewhat complacent, then I would suggest taking Paul's beautiful challenge in Romans to shake you out of your complacency: your capacity to excuse yourself and your sin as the Gentiles do in chapter 1, or to see yourself as superior to others and therefore self-righteous as the Jews do in chapter 2.

If, on the other hand, you feel that your situation before the Lord is peaceful, solid and somewhat deep, but that the need is to grow deeper, then I would take the beautiful first letter of John, which is really a summary of the whole Christian life. Basically John's letter has three or three and a half themes: that God is light and love, that we are darkness and lack of love, and, thirdly, that the only bridge between our darkness and God's light is Jesus Christ. What we might perhaps call the "half theme" is that the only test of our love for the Lord is fraternal love.

An Autobiographical Approach   You might choose whichever scripture passage helps you to the grace that you seek. The more autobiographical way of approaching this first week would be to first do a profile of yourself as you think God sees you, and then to listen to him, asking him to confirm or correct the profile. What I have in mind here is this: I have learned from experience, both as a pray-er and a director, that very often it is difficult for us to *listen* to the Lord. I mentioned on a cassette (*Prayer as Life and Growth*) that when we confess, we usually confess what *we* think God sees in us. How different it might be if we ask him to show us what *he* would like us to confess. What a tremendous grace it would be if we could see how he sees us instead of just evaluating ourselves according to his laws.

Yet, as people often say to me, how would we ever know how the Lord sees us? Well, I think that the greatest problem in listening is that our own self evaluations block the way. I have found the most effective way to avoid or to circumvent the problem is not to try to suppress my own self evaluation but to do it first and get it out of the way — to sit down as we begin this new day and reflect: What do I think God likes in me? That first. I find it better to begin with the "likes." Spend a whole hour or as long as necessary trying to think of everything that you think God likes in you. Note down the various positive points in your journal. If you find it hard to find anything he likes in you, that in itself is quite revealing. It shows you don't have a very good self-image and that you don't have a very positive image of God. In any case, really take the time to list all of the likes, all of the things you believe God likes in you. After a short break, do the same with the "dislikes." What do I think God dislikes in me? Try to list them all, large and small, everything you can think of.

When you finish this second list, take a short break again and, finally, come back for the third step in this more reflective part of the exercises to look over your two lists of the likes and the dislikes and try to rank them. Among the things God likes, which do you think he likes most, values most; which does he like, perhaps, but without considering them too important? I may be very gentle, but he may know that it is just a question of temperament. While he likes it, perhaps he doesn't get too excited about the fact that I am naturally sanguine. In the same way, rank the dislikes. Among all the things I think he dislikes in me, which do I really think he dislikes most? Which ones, perhaps, does he dislike the least? He may say, "Yes, you are timid, I know that; but it is your native temperament. I would be happy to change it, and in eternity we will change it, but it doesn't bother me too much. It is not a block to our loving relationship." Try then to rank all of the qualities, good and bad, as you think the Lord sees them in you.

You might say that all of this is not very prayerful. Indeed, it is more our own reflecting than listening to the Lord. But I think it can be tremendously fruitful. Many people have told me that it is the first time in their lives they have seen themselves "whole" and that it is a tremendously liberating experience. Moreover, the real praying begins once I have finished the profile. It might take the whole morning to complete your profile, but once you have finished then you can come before the Lord and say, "Okay, Lord. I've said everything I can possibly say. I can't think of anything else good or bad that I have not jotted down, that I have not confronted. Now, however, I come before you. This is the way I think you see me, but I don't know whether I'm right or not. So for the remainder of this first week, this afternoon and tomorrow, I will simply listen to you. Please correct or confirm whatever I have been able to say about myself."

My point is, I think we can listen much better after we are talked out. When people whom I don't know yet come to me for direction I find it is very important that I just listen patiently. Sometimes, indeed frequently, they can hear me only after they have talked themselves out. That is the concrete human experience which suggested to me that the same thing is probably true with the Lord. Note, however, that if you have done the profile and are now ready to listen, you have to be very patient because God speaks in silences, and he tends to be very, very slow! The first thing we realize is that we don't really know how to hear him. That in itself is a revelation: All these years I have been speaking of him, and I don't really know what he thinks of me!

It is at this point that you might introduce one of the three scripture selections that I mentioned earlier. If you are able to be still, to simply wait and listen and see where your thoughts and feelings lead you, fine. If, however, it is difficult to do so, then it might be helpful to read over whichever of the three scripture selections seems most appropriate to your situation. Note the lines or phrases in the chosen reading which strike or touch you. Live in the presence of these significant passages, see them in the light of your profile, and allow them to guide your listening. That really is the substance of the first week: the grace to see myself as God sees me.

As a final possible means to the grace sought, one could also use the five meditations that St. Ignatius suggests for the first week (paragraph numbers 45 to 71). As we said, they might be helpful as a means to realize the grace to see myself as he sees me. This is a third possible approach instead of or in addition to the scripture and the profile. Whatever helps to the grace is good.

Additional Directions: Flexibility, Moderation, Openness   Finally, it is helpful to note Ignatius' "additional directions" in paragraph numbers 73 to 90 in the *Exercises.* He gives practical guidelines concerning the use of light and darkness, the value of fasting and so on. They involve circumstantial details and should be applied flexibly, but I think they express a beautiful and very modern insight. Ignatius saw long, long ago what we are stressing to-

day, namely, that we are enfleshed spirits, that we
don't just pray with our souls or our heads but with
our whole being. When you see his stress on the use
of light and darkness and the need for flexibility concerning times, places and posture in prayer (he is in-
sistent on flexibility in posture, just as St. John of
the Cross is), you begin to realize his sense of our
embodiment. That we are not called to be angels is
very important to him and actually very important to
our prayer. So be aware of the fact that you pray with
your toes and your fingers as much as with your
soul. Maybe "as much as" is not a good phrase, but
the point is that you pray as a whole being, as an
enfleshed spirit. It is dangerous to try to "angelize"
your prayer.

St. Ignatius also has perceptive comments on
penance in numbers 73 to 90. The basic point he
makes is that penance is a *means* and not an end.
Thus in a retreat you should use penance (and everything else) insofar as it helps you to pray. The goal
here is to encounter God. Don't do penance for its
own sake or because somebody has told you it is a
good thing to fast in a retreat. It can be a very helpful means, but be flexible. Use it if it helps you to
pray better. If fasting leads me to spend all my time
thinking about my rumbling stomach, then I should
forget it. If it frees me to pray better, fine, then it
should be used. But, as St. Ignatius says, with moderation — and never as an end, but always as a
means.

To sum up, the basic principles he gives us are
flexibility and moderation, a great sense of the
uniqueness of the person that is myself, and there-

fore a great reverence for the mystery of God working in me. Not only are other people unique, but I
am too. I didn't come here to do some predeter-
mined, pre-cooked exercises. I came here for a vacation with the Lord. That means that he is the host.
Indeed the more I possess that listening attitude, the
more docile I can be to his leading, the more suc-
cessful this first week has been. The emptying of
myself of which we spoke is precisely a turning off of
my own noises, of my own voice, in order that I can
hear the still, small voice of God.

> The Lord said to him, "Go out and stand
> before me on top of the mountain." Then
> the Lord passed by and sent a furious
> wind that split the hills and shattered the
> rocks — but the Lord was not in the wind.
> The wind stopped blowing, and then there
> was an earthquake — but the Lord was
> not in the earthquake. After the earth-
> quake there was a fire — but the Lord was
> not in the fire. And after the fire there was
> a still, small voice. When Elijah heard it,
> he covered his face with his cloak and
> went out and stood at the entrance of the
> cave (I Kgs 19:11-13).

DAY THREE:

Victory Already Won in Christ

What We Have Discovered   As we begin day three of our eight-day retreat we recall that this day is a continuation of the first week, which we introduced yesterday. And the grace that we were seeking in the first week is to see ourselves as God sees us. To see and experience ourselves, because the type of seeing we have in mind here is a *felt* seeing, a seeing with the heart, we might say. I suggested yesterday several passages that we could use: the text of the *Spiritual Exercises,* paragraphs 45 to 71, where St. Ignatius gives the five traditional meditations for this first week which might be especially helpful for beginners, or Job, chapters 38 to 42, or the first epistle of St. John, or Romans, chapters 1,2,5,7 and 8. I also mentioned that one approach to the first week that I have found very helpful is to first do a profile

of myself as I think God sees me, listing in the journal the things that I believe he likes in me, the things
that I think he dislikes, and finally how I think he
would rank them. It is not, as we stressed, how I see
myself, but rather how God sees me. Thus the first
part of the profile, which is more meditative, more
your own talking and reflecting, should then lead
you to listen to the Lord. This can be done with the
help of some of the scripture passages which we
have mentioned, asking him as you read and reflect
to confirm or to correct your own profile of yourself.

We also stressed that in every day of the retreat
the test of the fruitfulness of our day, and the indica-
tion whether we should continue with the same
theme or move on to the next theme, is the grace
that we seek. Do I feel that the grace has been
given? For example, the grace that I seek in this first
week is to see myself as God sees me. This is, as we
mentioned, perhaps the most crucial part of the retreat, even though the second week, which is consid-
erably longer, is the heart of the retreat. This first
week is most crucial in the sense that if we can really
be naked and open before the Lord, then the rest of
the retreat follows more or less automatically. Since
the Lord desires our conversion far more than we do,
if we are open to that growth and that deepening, it
will surely come by his grace.

Against this background, I think that various
things may have happened as you prayed through
the second day yesterday. If, for example, in the profile you found it quite difficult to say what God likes
in you, if it was much easier to describe the negative
side than the positive, that very fact reveals some-

thing about yourself. It is quite likely that there are many negative points which God sees in you, but even in the worst of us there are also many things that he loves. If you found it difficult to articulate them, to affirm them, then it probably shows that you don't have a very good self-image and also that you don't have a very positive, loving picture of the Lord. In that case, it may well be that the greatest grace of your whole retreat will be to discover how understanding and tolerant and loving and positive the Lord is, and how patient. We don't do him a favor by denying or refusing to acknowledge the gifts he has given us.

If, on the other hand, you found it very difficult to see anything that was negative in yourself, that too might be quite revealing. What I would suspect that to mean is that you have a rather weak and un-developed sense of sin and perhaps a self-justifying attitude toward your life. Perhaps you see sin too ju-ridically, too legalistically, and you cannot see the real deeper demands of love. This challenge can turn us to chapters 7 and 8 of St. Paul's letter to the Romans, which I would like to comment on briefly for today.

Romans 7: Sickness and Promise   I think for committed persons the main problem is not sin as malice but sin as sickness. Thus for most people making a retreat like this the focus in seeing the negative aspect of ourselves will be on the things which we would like to uproot in ourselves and yet seem unable to change. For that reason, whichever of the passages you took for prayer yesterday, whether Romans or the first epistle of John or Job, I think it might be good to spend some time today on chapters 7 and 8 of Romans.

In Romans 7, one of the very few New Testament passages which does address itself to the problem, Paul confronts a basic difficulty that all of us have: We find within ourselves "two laws." He has been speaking in this letter about the law of Israel and how that law cannot save because, although it makes clear to us what is right and wrong, it does not give us the power to do the right. Somewhat hyperbolically St. Paul says that the person who knows the law, the Jew, is in a worse situation than the Gentile. Because the Gentile doesn't know all the obligations of the human person before God, he or she can find a partial excuse for sin in ignorance. On the other hand, the Jew knows from the law of Moses all that he or she should be doing. For this very reason, Paul says, he is in a way worse off because knowing what should be done he finds himself unable to do it. St. Paul's basic point is that justification comes from the saving grace of Jesus Christ and not from our own efforts to observe the law.

Very often Paul's writing is a stream of consciousness and one idea suggests another related idea. So here in chapter 7, verse 14 and following, the discussion of the Mosaic law leads him to another sense of law. He talks about the fact that even within himself a person ("I") finds two laws at work: the law of his flesh and the law of his spirit. He finds the good attracting him, he desires the good, and yet he finds himself unable to do it. He wants to follow God's law, especially the law of love, and yet he finds himself doing the opposite.

I think Paul here, as many commentators have noted, is speaking of "I" not as himself alone but as every human being. The point he makes is a crucial and troubling reality for every committed person who seeks to grow in God: There is another type of sin in us, sin as sickness, in addition to sin as malice. This is particularly evident in areas where instinct is very strong in us, such as vanity, envy, unchastity. It seems that despite the sincerity of our will our instincts are very difficult to control; they seem to go off in another direction altogether from what our will desires. In reflecting upon this wretched situation of the devout soul, Paul echoes the anguish in the heart of every committed person when he begins to question even his own sincerity. How can I say that I really want the good when I find myself doing something else?

Paul's answer to this is very beautiful. Toward the end of chapter 7 he says, "Who will free me from this body of death," from this inner tension that is tearing me apart? And his answer is, "Thanks be to God, through Jesus Christ our Lord." This is a very compressed way of saying, "Thanks be to God, the victory is achieved, is *already* won in Christ Jesus." We live in the already and the not yet. We find ourselves unable to do the good; yet by faith we know that Christ has already won the victory and that we will surely triumph if only we keep the faith. The devil, however, works in insidious ways to discourage us, to make us feel that our instinctual failings are a sign that we're far from God, that the whole struggle may be hopeless.

A little later we will talk about the rules which

St. Ignatius gives us for this first week for discerning the voices of the good and the evil spirits. But Paul here simply says that the victory is already won in Christ Jesus. The whole of chapter 8 is his expansion on that fundamental cry of triumph: When we do not know how to pray the Spirit of God prays within us. Whatever our human limitations, provided we live in faith and sincerely desire to love, the Holy Spirit is at work in us. Even when my prayer is most desperately dry, I can at least be the place where the God in me adores God the Father, where the spirit of God in my soul worships the God whom I desire to worship myself. It is a truly beautiful vision, and it ends with Paul's ultimate affirmation that *nothing* can separate us from the love of Christ Jesus. Neither life nor death, neither our own instinctual failings nor any of the frustrations of this world can really separate us from the love of God which is ours already in Christ Jesus. If your own experience yesterday and this morning has focused you on the awareness of your own sinfulness, not as malice needing to be forgiven but rather as sickness needing to be healed, then I would recommend that you spend some time today on these beautiful chapters of Romans 7:14 to the end of chapter 8, trying to let the triumphant affirmation of Paul echo in your own heart.

It is also possible, as I mentioned earlier, that some people can find it difficult to see themselves as sinful. If so, I think the reason is because they look at sin too juridically, too legalistically. Perhaps they have succeeded in their lives in observing at least the major commandments of the law; they are able to do well whatever is in their voluntary control and therefore they are complacent. Like the Pharisees, they do not find themselves in Romans 7. If that is the situation you find yourself in, perhaps it is a sign that your sense of sin is not very deep precisely because your sense of love is not very deep. A servant can be complacent because his obligations and rights are clearly spelled out. A friend can never be complacent because the limits of friendship are totally open-ended. There really are no limits to the love of friends.

I think this is why St. Teresa of Avila could consider herself to be the greatest of sinners. I used to wonder if she was exaggerating. But to do so doesn't seem in character for her, and now I believe that she really meant what she said. She knew that many people were doing things worse than she was doing, but she also realized that considering the love that God had shown to her she couldn't imagine anyone else similarly blessed responding as little as she had. Any of us who really live in love will have that same strong sense of sin that Teresa had. Nothing is small for those who love. While that does not mean that we are filled with anxiety and guilt, it does mean that there is a real undertone of sadness to our whole life, sadness that we cannot love as we are loved. We long for the time, probably only after death, when our instincts and our hidden vanities will be totally swallowed up in what our will truly desires.

The Discernment of Desolation   This ambivalent situation of the soul that loves and yet fails to love is a good introduction to the rules for discernment of St. Ignatius. For the first week, with its focus on self-knowledge, on my own sinful human situation before God, the rules appear in paragraph numbers 313 to 327 of the *Spiritual Exercises.* The second week rules (#328-336) deal more with the situation of someone whose life is already centered on Christ, as we shall see beginning tomorrow. One striking contrast between these two sets of rules is that the rules of the first week are almost entirely concerned with desolation, whereas in the second week the rules center totally on consolation.

Why is this so? I think the reason is because Ignatius sees the first week as the situation of beginners. We might say that it is the situation of conversion, of turning my life from centering on self to centering on the Lord. These conversions recur at a deeper level at various times in our life. There can be a new beginning, for example, when someone moves into the dry well in prayer, or when faced with a new challenge, such as marriage or religious commitment. All of these, as well as the initial beginning when we are first converted to the Lord, are times of beginning to live more deeply and authentically. At any time like this the rules for the first week are likely to be most appropriate.

What does Ignatius tell us in those rules? I would suggest that you read over numbers 313 to 327 sometime today. These rules are brief, yet they can be valuable guidelines for life. In the first two rules (#314-315) Ignatius indicates to us two different possible states of soul. If the soul is going from bad to worse, from mortal sin to mortal sin, then the devil will console us and the Lord will be the one who disturbs us. Whereas for the soul that is growing, that is going from good to better, even though there still may be many failings in our life, then the devil will be the one who disturbs us and the Lord will console us.

If we ask why this is so, in the seventh rule of the second week (#335) St. Ignatius explains more fully. The basic reason is because consolation is a way of encouraging us in our present course of action, while desolation is a way of calling into question our basic direction or commitment. When we are disturbed, desolate, anxious, we wonder if we are really on the right track. When we are consoled we feel confident that we should move ahead on our present course. So, in the situation of someone going from mortal sin to mortal sin, a spurious kind of consolation will be the devil's work because he doesn't want to rock the boat. He wants to preserve the person's basic orientation toward evil. In this case, the Lord will send desolation to call into question the sinner's very fundamental option. Whereas if somebody is going from good to better, the devil will try to disturb them and the Lord will encourage and console them.

Having made this distinction, St. Ignatius makes no further reference to the situation of someone going from bad to worse. All of the remaining rules presuppose the situation of someone seeking to grow and sincere in his or her commitment. Although Ignatius doesn't tell us explicitly I think this is because he would assume that anyone making a retreat, anyone committing himself or herself to this kind of search for God, surely belongs to that second group, the ones who are seeking to grow. He doesn't give us rules for people going from bad to worse because they don't seek guidance in growth and they do not make a directed retreat!

The next important point Ignatius makes (in #316-317) is that what we discern is our feelings of consolation and desolation. Desolation includes feeling states like turmoil, anxiety and restlessness, loss of faith, loss of hope, loss of love. Consolation is all that is opposite to desolation: joy, peace, tears of sorrow for sin, tears of gratitude because of the Lord's love in the passion. All of these are feeling states, and they are the raw material of discernment. That is why, as I mentioned earlier, we have to be in touch with our feelings if we are going to be discerning persons. In order to determine whether the Lord is speaking to us, we look in our journal for the feeling states which manifested themselves in our prayer.

For example, suppose that in trying to listen to the Lord yesterday afternoon after doing the profile you found yourself very restless, feeling the effort was fruitless since God seemed silent and nothing was happening. If because of this restlessness you shifted topics or got another book to read or tried to find some other way to escape from the restlessness, you would have made a decision in a time of desolation. All of your experience (the restlessness, the discouragement, the frustration) is a form of desolation.

How to Handle Desolation   Would you have acted correctly in thus turning away from the profile and the listening because of the desolation you felt? The answer is found in the basic guideline of St. Ignatius, perhaps experientially the most important of all the rules of the first week. He tells us (#318) to never, never make or change a decision in times of desolation. Why? Because for the committed soul desolation is never God's voice. Thus if someone did break off the prayer in restlessness, if he or she escaped from the silent listening and waiting because it seemed fruitless and restlessly shifted to something else, that would be a mistake. To repeat, desolation is never God's voice for those who are sincerely seeking him. So we should never make a decision at that time unless we want the devil as our spiritual director.

As St. Ignatius says in the following rules, in desolation we should persevere in the decision made when we were at peace. For example, we should follow the suggestions given for this first week if when we were still at peace they attracted us and appealed to us. He also tells us that we should pray a bit longer when we are desolate, rather than shortening our prayer. In this way we work against the enticements of the evil spirit. In addition we should do some penance if that helps us to discipline our restless feelings and instincts. And we should remind ourselves that desolation never lasts forever. It is an article of faith that God desires the salvation of each of us and that all we have to do is persevere in patience.

Ignatius also tells us in an important paragraph (#322) that there are three possible reasons why the Lord may *permit* (not cause) desolation. First, someone can be in desolation because of negligence, not as a punishment but as the Lord's way of waking us up, of shocking us into realizing that we are drifting and careless. But a person can also be in desolation even though he or she is truly generous and committed. Desolation is not, as good souls often take it to be, necessarily a sign that they have somehow failed God. Even the most generous of souls experience it. In such cases, Ignatius says this can be because the Lord wants to teach us that consolation is pure gift. As we mature that may be necessary, because at the beginning when our faith is weak and fragile he sometimes spoils us with consolation on demand, precisely because he is trying to win us to himself. As we become a bit stronger, though, we may find these earlier consolations much more elusive. God seems to be silent now when we are more deeply committed. He seems even to leave us to the disturbances of the evil spirit. Why? To teach us that consolation is gift, that he is the Lord of the encounter, not we.

Finally, Ignatius tells us that the Lord may permit desolation to "test" our love and fidelity. But "testing" here is analogous to the testing of steel by fire whereby all the impurities are burned away and the steel is made strong. Desolation purifies our love for God of all of the self-love that weakens it. It is easy to "love" when everything is beautiful, when I am getting a lot out of it. But I find out whether I *really* love precisely when the going is difficult.

Thus the Lord may permit desolation for various reasons. But he never causes it, it is never his voice; therefore we should never take it as a guide to action. He may permit it for reasons having to do with our negligence or to foster our growth in a fidelity that is already present and quite real. In any event, Ignatius insists that we should not decide or change a decision in desolation. And he seems to assume that desolation will be fairly common phenomenon in the first week. For example, since most of us are very busy, settling down to eight days of quiet is quite a change from our normal routine. Oftentimes our prayer life has suffered because of the busyness of our lives. Since we have become "surface" people, it can be quite hard to suddenly come to quiet, to turn from doing to listening. In such a case we may find ourselves very restless on these first two or three days of retreat. Since this restlessness is a form of desolation, we simply have to remember what Ignatius said: to persevere in the good resolution with which we began the retreat; to pray faithfully, if anything, to pray a bit longer than we had planned to; to bring some penance into our lives. In general, to say to the devil, and to our own selfish nature, "I am going to follow through on my commitment, and I have no intention of allowing you to discourage me and deflect me from it. If the Lord wants to tell me that I should forget about the retreat, that it's a mistake, fine! But he will have to tell me in peace, because I will not trust disturbance as a sign of his will. I'm ready to do anything, even to drop the retreat, but I will not believe that it is God's will to do so unless he tells me in peace."

It is helpful to recall here the masterful insight of C.S. Lewis, whose *The Screwtape Letters* is one of the 20th-century classics on discernment. In his book, Lewis tries to imagine himself in the situation of the devil, actually of a senior devil in hell named Screwtape who is advising his young nephew, Wormwood. The nephew, who is serving his apprenticeship here on earth, writes to the senior devil as his spiritual director to get advice on how to handle the various people that he has been assigned to corrupt. *The Screwtape Letters,* which records the "spiritual direction" by correspondence of this senior devil, Screwtape, to his nephew is very funny indeed. But at the same time it embodies a truly wise insight: Try to imagine yourself in the place of the devil. By so doing, you can gain considerable insight into your own areas of vulnerability. This will enable you to unmask the evil spirit and so to neutralize his attacks on you. Just think what you would do if you were a smart devil yourself. For example, if your disturbances made people pray longer, you would leave them alone quickly enough. But if by the disturbances you were able to shorten their prayer, then next time you would come back sooner with the same attack, knowing that you had your victim in your pocket.

Turning From Self to Christ: The Parable of the King   The first week then is a crucial time. It is not usually a joyful time in the sense that much of the second week can be, but it is a time when we can come to a real nakedness before the Lord. This experience brings a sober joy which perhaps even the second week cannot capture: a sense of liberation, of being clean, of being able to strip away the masks that each of us wears. And as we said, the criterion for loving from one week to another is the sense that the grace we seek has been realized. If you feel even by the middle of this third day that the grace of knowing and seeing yourself, of experiencing yourself as God sees you has been given, then it would be possible to move on into the second week. But if you feel that the grace you seek is still not fully realized, then spend the whole of this third day in prayer for that grace.

As I say, though, you may feel drawn to move on by midday. Thus it might be good if we briefly introduce the second week at this point. Once we stand naked before the Lord, in the second week we seek to be clothed with Christ — to put on the Lord Jesus, as St. Paul says. It is "to live, no longer I but Christ in me," as it is beautifully expressed in Galatians 2:20. As noted on the outline (see page 173) that really is the overall grace of this second week. We turn now from an honest and fruitful self-confrontation to a focusing on Christ. We desire that the emptiness in us may be filled with the Lord — that emptiness which we have been able to allow God to hollow out in us during the first week.

St. Ignatius introduces the second week with a famous meditation on the kingdom (#91 to 99 of the *Spiritual Exercises*). What he does there is to contrast Christ the King with a human leader. For example, here in the Philippines where I live and work and where we have recently faced a situation of crisis and great uncertainty, we might put the first part of the kingdom meditation as follows. Suppose a leader appeared who had the brilliant mind of our former president Marcos, the common touch of President Magsaysay, who was killed tragically in a plane crash almost 30 years ago, the legal and constitutional skills of some of our recent parliamentary leaders, the simplicity, modesty and strength of character of President Cory Aquino, and finally the sense of social justice of some of the Marxist leaders. Imagine that a man or woman appeared who combined all of these qualities in one person. Suppose he or she said to me, "I want to save the Philippines but I cannot do it alone. I ask you to join me in this crusade. It will not be easy. But I promise never to ask of you any sacrifice which I do not first make myself." Ignatius asks us: What would a Filipino worthy of the name respond to such a leader?

Then he says, let us compare this human ideal, which Cory Aquino approximates but which we may never see fully realized in practice, with the gospel picture of Jesus Christ. What kind of person is he? What does he offer compared to this ideal human leader? What does he promise? And what would any Christian worthy of the name of Christ respond to his invitation to join him in suffering and trial, to share his crusade to save not just the Philippines but the whole human race? Could any true Christian refuse to help in redeeming his people, especially since he promises us, as perhaps no human leader ever can, that he will never ask of us anything that he himself has not first undergone? Wherever we go and whatever we suffer, it will be different because we know that he has been there before us. As Hebrews 4:15 says, he has been tempted in every way that we are tempted.

Choosing a Gospel — and Writing One   The kingdom meditation is especially helpful for beginners who do not yet know the wonder of the person of Jesus. It situates in a context of challenge and invitation the gospel contemplations of the second week. We will develop this second week more fully in the next chapter. But I might mention now (since you may be ready to begin the new theme today) that I always suggest to retreatants that they choose just one of the gospels for their prayer throughout the second week. I realize that it is customary to suggest passages from different gospels for the various prayer themes. I myself, though, find it more helpful to choose just one of the gospels for the whole second week. My reason is this: I think each of the evangelists presents to us the Jesus whom he and the community from which he comes have experienced. Thus it can be much more fruitful for these few days that we can give to it to share one integrated and unified experience of the Lord.

How would you choose which of the gospels to use? If you do not have a favorite in mind, I might offer the following guidelines for choosing. I think the great point of St. Mark's gospel is the humanity of Jesus. The Jesus of Mark is the most human of the four, perhaps because it was written earliest when the church's reflection on Jesus' divinity was not yet so far advanced. This has great importance today when after several centuries we are finally coming to terms again with the humanity of Jesus, with his truly human consciousness, and with the fact that, as the letter to the Hebrews says, he has been tempted in every way that we are. So if you find that in your life Jesus tends to be rather remote, so divine that you find it difficult to identify with him in your own human temptation and suffering, then I would suggest choosing Mark.

St. Matthew's gospel is a magnificent total vision. For Matthew, Jesus is the new Moses and the church the new Israel. The whole of Israel's history is gathered up in Jesus. It is Matthew who lays particular stress on the fulfillment of scripture, of the Old Testament, in the events of Jesus' life. Matthew's gospel is also the most eschatological: The vision is from eternity to eternity. Thus it can be a very beautiful choice for someone who needs to see the larger meaning of the day-by-day events in which we tend to get lost.

By contrast, St. Luke's is the gospel of social service. It is also the gospel of woman: Woman plays a much more prominent part here than in the other gospels. I think both the stress on social service and the place of woman in Luke probably owe much to his own background as a Gentile and as a physician. He has the social concerns of someone who has given his life to serving the bodily needs of men and women. Luke's is also the gospel of the Holy Spirit, who plays a prominent role here as well as in Luke's *Acts of the Apostles.* But perhaps Luke is especially popular today because of his social concern. According to some commentators, even in the Our Father Matthew's Jesus is concerned about the bread that lasts forever, whereas Luke stresses the bread we need today. Both are essential dimensions. At different times in our lives we need to focus more on one or the other.

Finally, St. John's gospel is, I think, the gospel of contemplation. One of the great devices of John is what is called his irony. Throughout his gospel events have a double meaning: They mean one thing to God and another to men and women. The Samaritan woman in chapter 4 says, "Rabbi, give me this water to drink because I'm tired of coming to the well." She is thinking of the natural water of the well, while Jesus is thinking of a different water altogether. Similarly, in chapter 3 Nicodemus says, "How can a man go back into his mother's womb?" He interprets Jesus' reference to the need to be born again in a literal, naturalistic sense. After many similar misunderstandings in John, finally in chapter 11 Caiaphas says, "It is expedient that one man die for the people." And John tells us that Caiaphas did not know what he was saying. He spoke prophetically but he had no idea what his words really meant. With this repeated irony, John is telling us, I think, that contemplation is not seeing extraordinary things, seeing visions and hearing revelations. Rather, it is seeing the ordinary things through the eyes of God. That is why John is so deep; he takes us beneath the surface that we might see the very ordinary things of our lives contemplatively, as God sees them.

This brief description of the four gospels may help you to make your choice for this second week. Begin today with the prologue (Mark 1:1-13; Matthew 1 and 2; Luke 1 and 2; or John 1:1-18) and ask for the grace to accompany Matthew or Mark or Luke or John as they reminisce and share with us the Lord they knew in order that in our own lives we can write the fifth gospel ourselves. In the end, we cannot witness merely to Matthew's Jesus or Luke's. Ultimately we have to stand on the history of our own personal relationship to Jesus and our commitment to his kingdom. We have to write that fifth gospel. By the grace of God, these days will be an important chapter in the writing. Now that we are open, vulnerable, sensitive by the grace of the past three days, hopefully we can go much deeper in answering the all-important question, "Who is Jesus Christ for me?"

In view of all this, what can we say? If God is for us, who can be against us? Certainly not God, who did not keep back even his own Son, but offered him for us all! He gave us his Son — will he not also freely give us all things? Who can accuse God's chosen people? God himself declares them not guilty! Who, then will condemn them? Not Christ Jesus, who died, or rather who was raised to life and is at the right side of God, pleading with him for us! Who, then, can separate us from the love of Christ? Can trouble do it, or hardship or persecution or hunger or poverty or danger of death? (Rom 8:31-35).

DAY FOUR:

To Know More Intimately, to Love More Ardently

The Grace of the Second Week   As we begin this fourth day of our retreat, we are perhaps ready to begin also the second week of the *Spiritual Exercises*. In presenting the third day yesterday, I mentioned that in entering the second week our focus shifts from self-knowledge to knowledge of Jesus, and of God in Jesus Christ. For us Christians, the only way to know the Lord, to know God, is through Jesus. He is the way to the Father. And the only way for us to come to know Jesus, since we do not live in his time or place, is through the scriptures.

The gospels have been written, as St. John tells us at the end of chapter 20 (verse 31), precisely in order that we may believe. Just before that John has the beautiful incident concerning my namesake, doubting Thomas — an incident which used to make me very nervous when I was a young boy in parochial school. It always appeared as the gospel of the first Sunday after Easter. Since all of us parochial school students had to sit in the front of the church at the children's Mass, I always had the feeling that Jesus' rebuke (and the priest's homily) was directed personally at me.

But as I grew older and began to realize that Thomas' only problem was that he was absent when the risen Lord first appeared, and that he simply claimed "equal rights" with the rest of the apostles, I saw the incident in a better light. Later I came to realize that John puts this incident of the doubting Thomas at the very end of his gospel, precisely because *we* are those blessed ones to whom Jesus refers in speaking to Thomas, we who have not seen yet have believed. Immediately after the Thomas incident and Jesus' reference to the blessings of those who have not seen and yet have believed, John concludes his gospel (chapter 21 being a later appendix) with the words: "Many other things were done and said by Jesus which are not written down in this book, but these have been written in order that you (i.e., you blessed ones who have not seen) may believe . . . and that believing you may have life."

Thus the gospels are our way of coming to know Jesus; and through Jesus we come to know the Father. At this point in our retreat, having been able to open ourselves to the Lord and come to a deeper self-knowledge, we now seek in the second week to be filled with Christ. We pray that the emptiness that we have been able to allow the Lord to hollow out in us in the first week can now be filled with this Lord of ours, so that we may live no longer just ourselves alone but with Christ in us.

So the second week is really the heart of the retreat, and we can plan to spend at least the fourth and fifth and sixth days, and possibly part of the seventh day, in seeking its grace. We never know the Lord fully; we are never totally possessed by him until we are transformed and confirmed in grace. For this reason the process of putting on Jesus is a lifetime process. Every year we come back to the retreat, not merely to review the past and to scrape our souls clean, but to grow more deeply rooted in the Lord. We seek to allow him to penetrate into those corners of our lives which have not yet been filled with Christ in order to allow him to continue our conversion, since we are always *becoming* disciples.

That is really the dynamic of this second week of the *Spiritual Exercises*. The heart of the whole retreat is our desire to be filled with Christ and to discover where he is leading us now. What is his word to us is at this point in our lives? You recall that we said in the beginning that in a good retreat the Lord really has just one word or one message for us; it is in this second week that we hope to discover what this word of his is. The general grace that St. Ignatius gives us for all the meditations of this second week is his way of expressing the dynamic, creative power of God's word to us. He says we should seek to know him more intimately in order that we may love him more ardently and thereby follow him more faithfully. So the thrust is always apostolic. Our knowledge leads to love and love fructifies in action. Ignatius above all was an apostle, and his concern is not merely with a love which begins and ends in the feelings but with a love which, like St. Teresa of Avila's love, ends in action.

Selecting a Gospel and Dividing the Days

Toward the end of the third day, I indicated that I find it most helpful to choose a single gospel and to stay with that one gospel throughout the second week, and even the entire retreat. It has been customary in the past to select passages from various places in the scripture according to the topic under consideration. But I myself believe that it is much more helpful not to focus on various topics (for example, the vows), but to let one of the evangelists reveal to us the whole Christ as he experienced him in order, as we said, that we ourselves might write the fifth gospel in our own lives.

It has occurred to me that if we had only one gospel — suppose, for example, that St. Matthew's was the only one that survived — we would have assumed that Matthew's account was the "gospel truth" literally and factually. Actually with the four we cannot do that because they often differ in small details and sometimes even in important respects. Wherever Mark and Luke have one blind man or one beggar, St. Matthew always has two. The chronology of many events in Mark has been rearranged by Matthew and Luke so that the same passages and incidents appear in their gospels but in very different contexts and at different times. The human quality of Jesus in Mark, even to the point of his being angry and frustrated, is considerable toned down and "divinized" in St. Luke's accounts of the same incidents. Even the chronology of the passion in Matthew and Mark and Luke differs significantly from that in St. John.

Given these differences among the four gospels, we have to stop and ask what really is the intent, the factual character of these accounts of Jesus' life. Early in this century it was very fashionable to try to harmonize the four gospels into one coherent factual account to counter the modernist, rationalist attack on Christian faith. There was an attempt to use the very rational and scientific tools of the modernists precisely to prove that the gospels are strictly historical records. That is what led to the famous "lives" of Jesus by Father Prat and Archbishop Goddier and others. But, as we have come to realize in the light of differences such as those mentioned in the previous paragraph, it is really impossible to harmonize the four accounts at that level.

More positively, what we have come to realize and to cherish today is this: The reason we have four gospels is that each of their authors, coming out of different community traditions, is giving us not simply a scientific chronology of Jesus' life, but rather an account of how he or his resources *personally* experienced Jesus. They are not so much answering the question of who Jesus was in terms of time and place, although that is important enough as background; more central is the question: Who really is Jesus Christ *for me*? We contemplate Matthew's answer, and Mark's and Luke's and John's over the course of our lives in order that ultimately we may be able to give our own answer. That is what I meant in saying that the fact that there are four gospels points to the need for us to write the fifth gospel ourselves. When we come to judgment day we have to answer the question not who Jesus was for Mark but who Jesus is for us. From that perspective it is not disturbing but rather very beautiful and even necessary that we have four different canonical gospels.

I have suggested taking just one of the four for this retreat; and yesterday I suggested some criteria for choosing, if the Lord does not choose for you by strongly drawing you to one or the other of them. Over the course of our lives we come to know the Jesus of each of the evangelists as well as the Jesus of St. Paul. In that way, we gradually come to discover who Jesus Christ is for us personally.

On the outline which accompanies this book (see pages 173-175) I have indicated the prayer themes and graces for a retreat of 12 days. My intention is this: The longer time can be more fruitful, especially in this second week, since one could contemplate the whole (or most) of the public life of Jesus in the gospel chosen. If you can manage 12 days, then you could devote days four to nine to the second week, following the division indicated on the outline. But I also suggested on the outline how it could be adapted to the more usual length of eight days. Since eight days is the normal time allotted to a directed retreat today, let us base our discussion on that adaptation. In effect this means that it would be necessary to shorten the six days on the outline to three, or perhaps three and a half.

One way to do so would be this: If you are a beginner in the life of prayer, you could take days four, five and six on the outline. Those are the days with the subtitles, "The King Appears" (day four), "The

Kingdom Proclaimed and Discerned" (day five), and finally (day six) "The Mission." As a beginner you could focus on the parts of your chosen gospel that are given for those days. For example, for day four, today, St. Matthew, chapters 3 and 4; or St. Mark, chapter 1; or St. Luke, chapter 3, verse 1, to chapter 4, verse 13; or finally, St. John, chapter 1, verses 19 to 51. Any one of these could fit very well the theme of the appearance of the king. They also bring out the richness of the kingdom meditation, which St. Ignatius uses as an introduction to the second week and which I explained briefly at the end of day three.

If you are more mature in prayer, if there has been a time of growth and deepening already, and if your life commitment to the kingdom is already settled, then it might be more helpful to choose days seven, eight and nine on the outline. Day seven is entitled "The Challenge of Jesus," day eight "The Response to Jesus' Challenge," and day nine "The Church, Glory and Suffering." My reason for suggesting this approach for more mature pray-ers is this: Once we have accepted Jesus as king of our lives, once we have made the choice in our early years to follow him whether in celibacy or in marriage, that choice need not be repeatedly reevaluated or remade. It is continually reaffirmed, of course, but this is done in the very living of our chosen lives.

At that point in our maturing, a later part of the gospels, I think, will speak more to our present situation. There is, in fact, a transition from beginnings to maturity in the gospel narrative itself — in Jesus' formation of his first disciples. This can be seen in the famous passage (Mt 16:13-23 and parallels) where St. Peter answers in the name of the disciples after Jesus has asked, "Who do men say that I am?" Peter replies for them and for himself, "You are the Christ, the Messiah, the son of the living God." He accepts Jesus as the king of his life, as the longed-for Messiah of Israel. Jesus blesses him for speaking under the inspiration of his heavenly Father. But he then goes on to speak of the fact that this kingship of his, his messianic call, is going to be a call to suffer. He is to be the Suffering Servant of Isaiah, a figure whom the Jews could never identify with the Messiah. They knew those great chapters in Isaiah (42, 49, 50 and 52), but they never identified them with the longed-for Messiah whom they envisioned as a triumphant, political leader.

In his own person, Jesus is bringing together for the first time the Messiah, the anointed one of God, and the Suffering Servant of Isaiah. This is a great shock to Peter and he protests that it can never happen to his beloved Lord. As a good Jew he can't imagine the Messiah suffering and being rejected. But when Peter protests, Jesus reacts vehemently. He says, "Get behind me, Satan, because it is not God who is speaking through you now (as he was a few minutes ago), but 'man'!" This is not so much a personal attack on poor Peter; rather, Jesus is pointing out that Peter, who has just won a great victory in accepting Jesus as the Messiah, is immediately confronted with a whole new challenge to his faith — the challenge to surrender his own expectations and to accept Jesus as Messiah on Jesus' (and the Father's) own terms.

For those of us who are more mature in our prayer, I think it is more fruitful to focus on that second stage in Jesus' revelation of his own identity and of what it means to follow him. If you feel that your situation is similar to Peter's in Matthew 16, then for today you could focus on "The Challenge of Jesus," with the readings and the grace suggested on the outline for day seven. That means choosing either St. Matthew, chapters 11 and 12; or St. Mark, chapters 6:30 to 7:23; or St. Luke, chapters 11:37 to 12:59; or, finally, St. John, chapters 5, 7 and 8.

We might note that chapters 5, 7 and 8 of John form a unit. Chapter 6 seems to be out of place, perhaps because John's gospel was left unfinished when he died and the matter was not yet arranged in its final form. Chapters 5, 7 and 8, which are essentially Jesus' confrontation with the Pharisees, present a very strong challenge to our faith. I came to love John's gospel long ago, but the last chapters I learned to love were 5, 7 and 8. They seemed so stark, so strong, so confrontational: Jesus says, "I know the father and you do not!" Yet, at this point in my life, those might be my favorite chapters in John. There is something of a John the Baptist quality about them. As we mature, we are more able to take (and we even need) the raw confrontation with truth which these chapters demand. We are no longer so much in need of the gentle and indirect approach which beginners, perhaps, do require. Whichever one of the gospels we choose, the focus for mature pray-ers would be on this challenge of Jesus.

I should mention here that for each of the days of the retreat beginning from day one I have suggested a grace as the focal point of the day. For day one, you recall, it was to experience God's personal love and call as the foundation of my life. For days two and three, which we have just completed, it has been to see and experience myself as God sees me. As the outline indicates, I had the idea to suggest the grace by way of referring to a Pauline passage. This Pauline reference may be especially helpful in the second week. For today, day four, for beginners it would be to experience Ephesians 5:6-14; for those pray-ers who are more mature, who might be taking today what appears as day seven on the outline, the grace is to experience 2 Corinthians 1:15-22.

I have found since I had the inspiration to suggest the grace in this Pauline way, that often times these passages are very fruitful for prayer. Paul's "gospel" is of a different kind. He presupposes even the factual details of the evangelists, and he focuses almost totally on the question of who Jesus Christ is *for me*. Because of this subjective, personalist stress, Paul is usually difficult for beginners who do not yet know enough *about* the Lord to appreciate Paul's passion for him. Yet, as we grow, as the Jesus of the gospels becomes more and more real to us, we learn to love Paul. We come to find an echo of our own experience in his more subjective expression of who Christ is in his life. In fact, pray-ers sometimes find, especially as their prayer matures and they move more into the dry well, that just the Pauline passage given as the grace can be quite sufficient for the prayer of the whole day. That provides a fifth alternative approach, in addition to selecting one of the four gospels.

Let me repeat what I said at the beginning: Use as much or as little of the scripture and of the other suggested readings from the *Exercises* and from books like Stanley as helps to the grace that you seek. The important thing is the grace; whatever means help us to that grace are good. If we find that we need very little reading, that for example just those few lines of Paul are quite sufficient for the whole day, that is fine also.

Discerning the Work of the Good and the Evil Spirits   As we move into this fourth day and the second week, it will be helpful to continue the explanation of discernment which we began yesterday. Since the retreat is a school of prayer, and may also be a time of decision, Ignatius sees discernment as central to the whole experience. We discussed a number of his first-week rules yesterday, and we pointed out that in this week Ignatius' focus is entirely on desolation. Rules 10 and 11 (#323-324) refer to consolation but they do so merely to contrast it with the alternating experience of desolation. So the real focus in this first week is on the experience of desolation. As we explained yesterday, that is because this is the way the evil spirit normally works on beginners: by homesickness, discouragement, restlessness and the like. We also stressed that desolation is never *caused* by God, and for that reason we should never make or change decisions concerning our commitment to our Lord in times of desolation.

But the obvious question still must be asked: Why does God *permit* desolation? Even if he doesn't cause it, still our faith tells us that nothing can happen which is beyond his control. Even the devil is not a free agent able to work independently of God. He is a creature like us. So, even if the Lord never causes desolation, and even if we should never allow it to guide our decisions, we still have to ask why he allows it. As we say yesterday, St. Ignatius replies to this question (#322) by giving three possible reasons why the Lord may permit desolation. Since his doctrine has great practical importance in a life of prayer and in a good retreat, let us recall and develop a bit more fully these three reasons.

First, Ignatius mentions that we may have desolation because we ourselves have grown negligent or tepid. We may have entered into the retreat, for example, with reservations, holding back, unwilling to put our whole life before the Lord. We may want to make a retreat, but at a level of mediocrity which will not disturb certain attachments and certain patterns of action in our life. In this case, the Lord may allow desolation not to punish our negligence but to wake us up. He doesn't cause it, but as in the book of Job, Yahweh may permit Satan to work in our lives for various reasons of his own, quite different from the reasons of Satan. While Job is not negligent, his story does make clear the contrasting purposes of which we speak. Satan's purpose in testing Job is to shake his love and fidelity and to prove that he is no better than anyone else. As becomes clear at the end of the book, God's reasons for allowing Satan to work are quite different. Contrary to the evil spirit's intent, the very desolation which Satan inflicts on Job has the effect of transforming and deepening Job's love. Similarly, if we are negligent, as Job was not, desolation may be permitted by the Lord to wake us up and to bring us back to our senses.

It is very important to recall, however, that desolation comes to the lives of the most committed people and not only to those who are negligent. The second and third reasons for desolation, which Ignatius gives in number 322 of the *Spiritual Exercises*, both refer to committed souls who are not negligent. To put very briefly and simply what St. Ignatius says there, the Lord may allow desolation and permit the evil spirit to disturb us, first of all to teach us that everything — consolation, peace, joy, all the good things in our life — is pure gift. We cannot produce consolation by finding the right breathing exercises or the right guru or the right techniques of meditation. If we could do so, the consolation would be our own production. It would in the end be a fruit of our own imagination. No, God is not the product of our own efforts. He is free and sovereign — he is Lord! So he permits desolation to make us realize that consolation is his pure gift and that we can only wait on his giving.

Ignatius stresses this point very strongly. At the same time, he says that the Lord also permits desolation in order to test our love. I think the point of this "testing" is to purify, the way steel is tested by fire. Committed souls learn to love much more deeply in the hard times. In the marriage ceremony the spouses promise fidelity "for better or worse." In the better, they learn the joy of loving; but in the worse, in desolation, they learn to love unselfishly. I think it is in that sense that our love is tested in the "worse" of desolation, like steel by fire. All the impurities of selfishness, timidity and so on are burned out of it and our love becomes very strong.

This purifying, strength-testing of love is, I believe, the basic reason for the desolation of Job. Satan tempts him in order to shake his love, but by the end of the book exactly the opposite effect has been achieved. Far from being shaken in his love, Job is much deeper. So much so that he can say, in chapter 42, "Until now I have only known you by hearsay; only now, after this time of purgation and desolation, do I begin to see you face to face." Desolation has healed Job's eyes and purified his soul and made it possible for him to begin truly to know God.

Who the Devil Is Like   With this background concerning the divine meaning of desolation, it will also be helpful to read over the three famous analogies which St. Ignatius gives in the *Spiritual Exercises,* in paragraphs 325, 326 and 327. He compares our enemy, the evil spirit who tries to disturb our peace, 1) to a nagging woman who in his image is physically weaker than the man and therefore has to get her way by psychological warfare; 2) to a false lover, the man who persuades his girl friend to secrecy when he is deceiving her and abusing her love; and 3) to a military commander. Just as the nagging woman achieves by psychological manipulation what she cannot achieve as physical force, so too the evil spirit is weak when we are strong, but ruthless when we are timid and vacillating.

And like the false lover, he always persuades us to secrecy. "Don't discuss your problem with a spiritual director because they're all too busy." "Don't open your doubts and difficulties to your superior or to someone who can help you because they're too narrow-minded." The devil presents all sorts of reasons to prevent us from being open. He does that because he cannot stand the light of day. Once we speak honestly to someone, as I find in my own experience as a director, the problem is often dissolved in the very sharing. Sometimes, the director doesn't even have to give advice or comment because in the very process of opening it up, of dragging the problem out into the light of day, the person discovers that the answer is already clear. Surely the false lover knows that if the girl ever reports to her brother or her father what he is doing, what they are doing together, his deceits will be quickly unmasked. So he says, "Don't tell your father; he's too narrow-minded. Your brothers are too old-fashioned. Just keep it a secret between us."

Finally, St. Ignatius says that the devil is like a military commander: He attacks us where we are weak and not where we are strong. He is not a fool. He surveys the ground, he knows our own vulnerabilities. I think that with good people, devout people, the devil is quite willing to have us emphasize the areas where we are already strong. In our confessions, for example, he is willing to urge truly charitable persons to confess every least little failing against charity, to become more and more punctilious, and more and more sensitive to the tiniest failing in their areas of genuine strength, as long as he can thereby induce them to ignore the areas where they are vulnerable. Such a person may be struggling to be more and more charitable and all the time be timid or compromising. "Charity" becomes a mask for lack of courage to take a stand. The devil is willing to encourage that kind of virtue. Like a military commander he wants to keep the weak wall of the fortress unrepaired. He is willing to encourage us to concentrate our energies on building the sturdy walls higher and higher, as long as he knows the weak wall is untouched and he can come in at any time he wants.

This, in substance, is what Ignatius has to say about discernment for beginners. As we mentioned, such beginners may not be only those just starting to live an interior life, because we experience several "beginnings"; for example, when we are called to a new state of life, or when we are drawn to a new kind of prayer, especially when we move into the dry well. The whole "dark night" experience of St. John of the Cross is, I believe, an example of the desolation which Ignatius describes. And it happens at this time because in a real sense we are then beginning again. In fact, John often calls those entering the dark night "beginners." They are moving into a strange new world, and the devil works overtime to turn them away from this new challenge.

The Two Standards: A Foundation for Discernment   Before we finish this presentation for the fourth day, I will introduce the second of the great thematic meditations which St. Ignatius provides as a framework for the second week. In a 30-day retreat it comes on the fourth day of the second week (*Spiritual Exercises* #136-148) and it is traditionally called the meditation on the "Two Standards," the two flags. In the medieval concept of warfare, which St. Ignatius knew firsthand since he himself had been a soldier, the most important person in the whole army was the flag-bearer. This was because, in the highly formalized and traditionalized battle array then prevalent, every warrior had his own place. Each one's position was determined in relationship to the flag-bearer. Thus, to be sure he was in the right place, all he had to do at any time was to look around and see where he was positioned with respect to the flag, the standard, which was held aloft by one of the soldiers. If the flag-bearer was killed, the army had no center; the soldiers had no point of reference, and defeat would almost surely follow.

St. Ignatius uses this classic, medieval picture to suggest to us a reflection on the spiritual warfare in which we are engaged. His point is that there are two celestial armies: the army of Christ and that of Satan. Therefore there are two standards, two flag-bearers, each holding aloft a standard which identifies the army to which he belongs. The standard of Satan has on it, "riches, honors, pride" — riches, leading to honors, leading to pride. The standard of Jesus Christ has written on it, "poverty, humiliations, humility." Now the point of Ignatius here, which is often misunderstood, is *not* to choose between the standard of Christ and the standard of Satan. That would not make much sense when one is already in the middle of the second week. No one should be making a retreat, and no one should have persevered in the retreat for four or five days already (or 12 or 13 days in a 30-day retreat), if he or she has not chosen yet between Christ and Satan! That should have been settled long before.

The point of the two standards is not choice but *discernment.* It has to do with our growth in Christ at this time in the retreat and at this stage of our life. The point St. Ignatius is making is that even committed souls, such as he presupposes the retreatants to be, can easily drift into the wrong army. Even with all the good will in the world we can find ourselves standing under the standard of Satan. Not that we deliberately choose him, but in the confusion of battle it is easy to end up there. To prevent this from happening, Ignatius tells us, we must look from time to time and see what flag is flying over our head. If we find ourselves under the flag that says "riches, honors, pride," then we can be pretty sure we have drifted into the wrong army, that somehow we have allowed ourselves to be converted by the world which we set out to convert. On the other hand, if we look up and see overhead the standard which says, "poverty, humiliations, humility," then our situation, painful as it may be, is tremendously reassuring. It means that we are in the right place, that we stand under the flag of Christ, that we are fighting in his army.

This meditation of Ignatius, the second of the great thematic meditations after the kingdom, is the basis of all discernment. He suggests it to us as a background consideration as we move more deeply into the second week. Thus you can pray over those numbers (136-148) in the *Spiritual Exercises* directly if you wish, or you could simply keep in mind what I have said above and what Ignatius says in the text as a sort of background as you continue to contemplate the life of Jesus. Notice how the two standards, the two armies, confront one another in the gospel; see Jesus himself taking a stand vis-a-vis Satan. Consider not so much how we choose between them, but how you may become so filled with the values of Christ that you can readily discern between the two value systems even after you have chosen.

We recognize the danger that we, with all good will and with much experience, can end up in the wrong army. Even now and in the future, you could find yourself standing under the wrong flag. As you contemplate the Lord today — his love for the Father, his values, his call to you — ask for the grace to be truly discerning. We have already spoken about the discernment of desolation; in the days to come we will have more to say about the discernment of consolation. But basic to all discernment is this meditation on the two standards, the contrasting values of Jesus Christ and of Satan. We have chosen Christ, but that choice has to be lived concretely in faith. And we need a guide to be confident that we are still on the side of the good angels.

> You yourselves used to be in the darkness, but since you have become the Lord's people, you are in the light. So you must live like people who belong to the light, for it is the light that brings a rich harvest of every kind of goodness, righteousness and truth. Try to learn what pleases the Lord. Have nothing to do with the worthless things that people do, things that belong to the darkness. Instead, bring them out to the light. . . . And when all things are brought out to the light, then their true nature is clearly revealed; for anything that is clearly revealed becomes light. That is why it is said,
>
> > "Wake up, sleeper,
> > and rise from death,
> > and Christ will shine on you"
> > (Eph 5:8-11,13-14).

DAY FIVE:

To Follow More Faithfully

Gathering Up the Threads   As we begin day five of our vacation with the Lord, it might be helpful to recall how far we have come. We first spent a day painting in the background of God's love, acknowledging the principle and foundation of our lives. We saw and affirmed that the only end for which we are made is the glory of God and our own salvation, and that everything else is a means to this end. For those of us who are apostles and those who are called to live in the world, our own salvation involves the salvation of others also. But, strictly speaking, even the salvation of others is a means for us. God is their savior. If he chooses to work through us, that is of course joy and gift. But they belong to him, for the end is God's glory and our salvation.

With that as background, beginning on the second day we focused on the call of God, the word of God to us at this point in our lives and at this moment of the retreat. As I suggested earlier, I firmly believe that in a good retreat the Lord has just one message for us. The basic pattern of that message we know: that knowledge of God and knowledge of self go hand in hand. Therefore, there can be a structure to our retreat without in any way binding the Spirit or restricting his freedom to work in us however he chooses. In this spirit we prayed for the great grace of seeing ourselves as God sees us at this point in our lives. This was the grace and gift we sought in the first week of the exercises, essentially on the second and third days of this eight-day retreat.

Now, having been able to come naked before the Lord, we seek in the second week, which we began yesterday, to be clothed with Christ. We pray that the emptiness in us may be filled with him, that we may "put on the Lord Jesus." This second week is the heart of the *Spiritual Exercises,* as we said. If the first week is made well, if we really have been able to see ourselves as God sees us, then the rest of the retreat follows fairly surely. The heart of the retreat, however, is still the second week. Here we contemplate Christ in his own public life in order to discover more deeply who he is for us and what it means concretely to follow him, to be filled with him.

Thus a retreat can be a time of decision — to chose a state of life, for example. Among the authorities on the *Spiritual Exercises* there has been considerable discussion whether a retreat is primarily a school of prayer, as scholars like William Peters would say, or whether it is primarily a time of election or decision concerning God's will for our lives. The latter was the view of the great Jesuit historian, Hugo Rahner. I myself feel that it can be either. At certain turning-point times in our lives, the retreat will be focused on the choice of a new course of action: perhaps a new vocation, or a new decision within that vocation, a change of mission and so on. At other times, though, when there do not seem to be any big decisions to be made, the retreat may well be more properly a school of contemplation, a school of prayer. Even when the retreat is a school of prayer, however, since praying is loving, and since love shows itself in deeds and not merely in words (as we shall find St. Ignatius stressing at the very end of the exercises), there will always be some sort of commitment involved. It may not be a new decision; it may be simply a call to a deeper trust, or a deeper love.

So in this second week St. Ignatius presents us with the four great thematic meditations which form the background for our contemplation of Christ's life. We don't meditate on or contemplate the gospels merely to get to know them better, but with a view to following Jesus more closely. As we have seen, the kingdom meditation presents the beginner with the choice of either following this divine king, with all that he offers and all that he promises and all that he challenges us to, or following a human "king," a human ideal with all the offer and promise and challenge which that brings.

We have also seen yesterday in the second great thematic meditation, that St. Ignatius presents to us a deeper challenge, the two standards or the two flags. His image here is based upon medieval military practice, where the armies fought under a flag in formation and the flag-bearer or the standard-bearer was the crucial figure in the whole formation. The soldiers took their positions — knew they were in the right place — by looking up to the flag and checking where they stood in respect to it. St. Ignatius presents us, as we saw, with the flag or the standard of Christ: poverty, leading to humiliations, leading to humility; and the standard of Satan: riches, leading to honors, leading to pride. As I stressed yesterday, his point is not that we choose between Christ and Satan, which would be rather foolish and redundant for someone serious enough to make an eight-day retreat.

No, his point is deeper: The two standards provide the basic foundation of the whole art of discernment. Even when we are committed to the Lord it is still possible to drift into the wrong army. Even when we have made our commitment, have given our "yes" to Christ, the battle is still a confused one. Our war is not against flesh and blood but against principalities and powers who are shrewder than we are. So discernment is always necessary to discover and to reassure ourselves that we still stand with Christ. If the flag under which we find ourselves fighting bears the legend "poverty, humiliations, humility" — if it corresponds to Jesus' response to Satan's temptations in Matthew 4 or Luke 4, rather than to the temptations of Satan himself as cited in the same passage — then we can be confident we are still with the Lord.

As we mature in our commitment, the challenge that confronts us becomes more subtle, as we shall have to explain shortly. Today we will consider St. Ignatius' famous (and often misunderstood) discussion of discernment as a tool for election or decision-making. Then tomorrow we will explain the rules for discerning consolation. This is a more difficult art then discerning desolation because, as we grow and as we become committed, the devil has to work in subtler ways to deceive us. The cruder forms of desolation which disturbed and shook us when we were beginners will no longer have that much power over us. We have now in some sense seen the Lord. We are convinced of his importance to our lives. So the devil, to seduce us, has to mimic the voice of God. Since he cannot tempt us grossly and by crude disturbances, he has to come under the guise of good.

Before considering the role of discernment in the making of retreat decisions, let us recall what we stressed earlier: the importance in the retreat of going at your own pace. I have been suggesting a certain flow of days and weeks here, but Ignatius is convinced — and he wants us to be convinced—that the important thing within this general flow is to follow the movement of grace. So move at the pace which you find natural and fruitful. The one restriction Ignatius imposes is that we should not go *ahead* of the theme or the topic presented. In general, follow this restriction faithfully. There could be times when someone might shorten one part of the retreat in order to give more time to something to come. But unless your own prayer life is quite mature, be careful not to do it without the guidance of a good director. In that case, of course, it could be done provided that you are also open to the guidance of experience. If you find the Lord seems to be resisting your moving ahead, be humble enough and realistic enough to step back and slow up the pace.

Generally speaking, then, and especially for beginners, the norm Ignatius gives us would be not to move ahead of the theme or the topic or the grace presented. On the other hand, it is always good to look back. I even suggested that we make the final prayer of each day a repetition of the whole day, or perhaps of all the days of the retreat up to this point. In this way, we seek to tie together the threads of the tapestry that God is weaving in our lives and in the retreat. We are always seeking to see the unity of the experience thus far.

To summarize, looking back is good; going slower than the pace presented is fine, especially if it seems that the Lord wishes you to spend longer on some particular grace or topic. But jumping ahead, generally speaking, is not such a good idea.

Three Kinds of Persons   As we move into this fifth day of our retreat, we should next speak about the guidelines which Ignatius gives us for making a good "election." Frequently, although not always, some decision, some choice, some important discernment will be called for at this time in the retreat. St. Ignatius gives us the third of the great thematic mediations as a background for this choice or deeper commitment. It is known as the three classes of men (or women) and is found in paragraphs number 149 to 157 of the *Spiritual Exercises,* right after the meditation on the two standards. Here again St. Ignatius gives us a background reflection on the different dimension of our commitment. If the kingdom represents the fundamental choice, and the two standards represents the importance of discernment in adhering to that choice, then the three classes of persons basically tells us this: If we are committed to the Lord as St. Ignatius presupposes that we are, still there are degrees and levels of commitment.

He introduces his parable by saying (#149), "This is a meditation . . . to choose that which is better." We have here a famous Ignatian theme: I don't want to do merely the good, but the better. I want to choose not only what is good and legitimate, but what is for the *greater* glory of God. The story he tells (#150) "is the history of the three classes of men. Each of them has acquired ten thousand ducats (we can say, ten thousand dollars), but not entirely as they should have, for the love of God. They all wish to save their souls and find God our Lord in peace by ridding themselves of the burden arising from the attachment to the sum acquired, which impedes the attainment of this end."

Let us review the situation. Each of these persons has acquired ten thousand dollars. They don't seem to have acquired it dishonestly; it is not stolen, so there is no obligation of restitution in question. But at the same time they have not acquired it in an ordered way, that is, for the love of God. Let us say, for example, that they have worked hard to acquire it or they have taken a ticket in the lottery or the sweepstakes and they have won the ten thousand dollars, thinking of all the things they would do once they won it. It is legitimately theirs, either by work or by luck. But God played very little part in acquiring it for all of them. Moreover, it is also true of all of these men that their hearts are in the right place. They wish to save their souls; they want to find God in peace. They all recognize the problem that this money is an obstacle, that they have an attachment to the money and they can't really be free for God until they are free from this attachment. Notice that we are dealing here with committed people in the sense that, although they are going to react very differently to the challenge that is presented to them, each desires to do the right thing before God.

How then do these three classes of people differ? The first group, as Ignatius says in 153, would like to rid themselves of the attachment they have to the money in order to find God and save their souls. But they never get around to taking any concrete action. The hour of death comes and they have not made use of any means to get free of the attachment. We could call them mañana people. That is, they want to be free for God, but they postpone acting until tomorrow. The problem is, as Ignatius points out to us, that tomorrow never comes. It is always today. So their wishes never lead to any action. If wishes were horses, beggars would ride. If wishes were actions, these people in the first group would be saints.

The second group, by contrast, want to be free of the attachment and they also recognize, as the first group does not, that tomorrow will never come. But they wish to be free in such a way that they retain what they have acquired. God is to come around to what they desire. They want him to will their attachment so it no longer remains a disordered one. For example, they want to marry Joe, and then they spend a great deal of prayer time convincing God to tell them to marry Joe so that they can console themselves that it is his will. The problem is, as Ignatius says, that they do not really get free of their attachment in order to go to God.

If the first group are mañana people, always postponing a decision until tomorrow, the second group could be described as the tithers, the ten-percenters. They give God something. They do try to involve him in their decision, but they bargain with him. They may even give 20 percent to Catholic Charities — in order to have the free use of the other 80 percent! They bargain with God in order to induce him to allow them to do what they wanted to do all along. They try to keep him quiet with the 20 percent so he won't interfere with their plans for the other 80 percent.

The Ignatian Deal   I mentioned the example of marrying Joe. It is important to see that the "ten thousand dollars" here may not be money; it can be friendship, or career, or *anything* to which I am attached — anything whose possession I have come into without really considering the glory of God, and thus anything that blocks my full freedom to follow him. Whatever the attachment may be, the third class (the Ignatian ideal) are those who want to rid themselves of the attachment, and in such a way that they desire neither to keep nor to give up the ten thousand dollars. Their only desire is to do whatever the Lord wants, whatever is for his greater service and praise. It is important to notice that, contrary to what we might expect, persons of the third class do not necessarily give up the ten thousand dollars. If they did simply give it away, it would still be *they* deciding.

St. John of the Cross tells us that the attachments that are most dangerous for devout people are their pious attachments, not their attachments to money and possessions, but to their devotions, their consolations, or their apostolic works. For example, someone can be in the seminary or convent not because God has called them, but because they want it. Since their attachment appears to be very pious, they may deceive themselves. Even directors who are not very perceptive may also be deceived. Strange as it sounds, such people may choose, for example, the priesthood without even considering God's will. They give their life to God whether he wants it or not. While they do give the "money" away, they are still the ones deciding how to dispose of it.

The third kind of person is quite different: He or she places the whole attachment on the table before God and says, "Lord, there is the ten thousand dollars, my life, whatever I am attached to. I place it all before you. What I ask is that you show me how to dispose of it, that your will and my will may be one. If you want me to keep the whole ten thousand, fine, as long as that is what you want and it is to your greater glory. If you want me to give the whole sum away and not know where my next meal is coming from, that's also fine, as long as it is what you want. If you want me to give 20 percent away and keep 80, that's fine also."

The question then is not what I do with the money, but *who* decides. This is why you find saints in situations of power and wealth. You don't find many of them; but then again you don't find many saints anywhere. They can be found even in affluence, though, because the question is not what they have or do not have, how poor or rich they are, whether they are vowed or married or whatever. The question rather is: Who decided? Is it the Lord who led them to this choice, this state of life, these possessions or this lack of possessions?

We talk much today of a preferential love for the poor, which is a very good thing inasmuch as it works against our natural inclination to favor the rich, to be seduced by secular standards of success and value. But we have to be very careful what we mean, because the poor are not all saints either. The real crucial test of sanctity is: Who really is the Lord of one's life? I think in many ways it is easier for the poor to be detached because they have fewer possessions to be attached to. But the trouble is that they can be attached to their fantasies and desires just as much as wealthy persons are attached to what they actually possess. The challenge of the third class is to lay my whole life — my desires as well as my possessions — before the Lord.

It is also good to note that religious and priests are going to find it just as difficult as others to be men and women of the third class. Very often we too find ourselves in the second class: We also bargain with God. But strangely enough, at times we who are vowed to the Lord give him 99 percent and keep for ourselves only one percent. We give away by our vows all the important things to which most people cling: the right to possess, the right to marry, the right to be self-determining. Then we hide 20 or 30 dollars under the mattress to be sure that we are protected against some unreasonable superior. In a way we are more foolish when we do that than the person who gives away 20 percent and keeps 80. We also are trapped in the second class, but at least those who give away 20 and keep 80 percent have something to show for their timidity, for their refusal to grow! We are foolish because we give away all the things that might be considered worth clinging to only to get ensnared by something that is hardly worth it.

So the third class is a very high and very beautiful ideal. It is rarely realized in any state of life, but at the same time it is possible if we desire it and allow the Lord to set us free. It is really God's gift. Ignatius values it so highly precisely because this freedom from our attachments is an essential precondition of genuine discernment. When we seek to discover God's will, we all realize that authentic discernment is difficult. Now, perhaps, we can see more clearly why this is so. It is because we cannot make ourselves free just by our own efforts from all the other "noises" in us. We tend to rationalize our attachments. For example, a religious fanatic is someone who is attached to his or her own will and has baptized it with the name of God. People who are very rigid in their religious practices, in their attachment whether to the old ways or to the new, are people who cling to their own "possessions" in a deceptively pious way. They fight for the old church (or the new) to which *they* are attached, and their war is waged in the name of God!

Because the ways in which the heart of man can block discernment and confuse the issue are so subtle, St. Ignatius tells us, in a section toward the end of this second week (#170 ff.), that in making a good choice we must be clear about means and ends in our life. There is a strong echo of the third-class ideal when he says that we must choose the end first, and then choose the means insofar as they help us to that end. We must not, that is, choose the means first and then try to twist them to the end. He says some people choose marriage, which is a means, and then having chosen marriage they try to figure out how to serve God within the married state. I suppose we could say that most *good* people act in this way most of their lives. It happens also in religious life. Devout people do it with assignments and jobs. They are determined to be in a certain place or have a certain career, so they do everything to bring about their desire, and then they try to serve God in the choice they have made. The inversion of end and means, which is the problem of the second-class person, vitiates their discernment.

Three Occasions for a Good Choice   So, as we continue to contemplate Christ's life in this second week, you can see that Ignatius presents us with a very large challenge. But it is a challenge which the *Spiritual Exercises* themselves are designed to meet. He goes on to say (#175-177) that, assuming that we have the proper disposition to hear God, we can discover his will in one of three ways, which he calls three occasions for making a good choice. First of all, I can choose God in what I have called a time of revelation, where God's will is so clear that I cannot doubt what he desires. St. Ignatius mentions the vocations of St. Paul and St. Matthew as examples of this revelation time (see Acts 9:3-6 and Mt 9:9). In such cases there is no discernment because God's will is clear-cut.

Ignatius also mentions (#177) a time when God seems to be silent, a "time of tranquility" he calls it, when we don't get any clues from the Lord as to what he would like us to do. In such cases there seems to be no word of the Lord to discern, and so "we freely and calmly make use of our natural powers." Sometimes this happens because the Lord does not wish us to be lazy; he desires us to use the intelligence and training and the background which he has given us. In such cases we come before him really open and detached. We say, "Lord, what would you like?" But he seems to be off on the other side of the world, totally uninterested in our decision.

If that happens, it may well be because he wants us to do our own share of the work first. So St. Ignatius mentions that, in those situations where God is silent and we don't have anything to discern, we should use our natural powers to discover his will. In numbers 178 and following he mentions two ways of doing so: one more meditative or analytical, and the other more contemplative or imaginative. We can proceed meditatively by weighing the pros and cons, using our analytical reasoning to line up all the reasons for and against the possible choices and determining where the preponderance of evidence points. We can also proceed more imaginatively, more contemplatively. I can do this by imagining what I would advise someone else who came to me faced with the same decision. Or I can imagine myself on my death bed or at the final judgment and discover what I would wish to have chosen then. But at the end of these ways, whether we use the imagination or the understanding to come to a decision in this natural way, we should then propose it to the Lord and ask him to confirm it if it really is his will.

How does he confirm it? The answer brings us to the final occasion for making a good choice (#176). Ignatius tells us we have to "read" the movements of the diverse spirits (the consolations and desolations) in our prayer. Actually he is extremely brief on this point. All he says is that at this time "much light and understanding are derived through the experience of desolations and consolations and the discernment of diverse spirits." We have already said something about desolation and about discernment in general, and tomorrow we will speak about the discernment of consolation. But the reason for Ignatius' brevity in this number is because his reference to discernment points to the rules for discernment which, as we have seen, come later in the book (#313 ff.). His point here is that we do not normally get a clear revelation of God's will, although that can happen. Usually we have to use our own heads (our reasoning and/or our imagination) first. Even then the key to discernment is not our own reasoning but rather our experience of consolation and desolation. And these, as we have seen, are feeling states. So discernment is really reading, interpreting our feelings.

We will come back to that tomorrow, but as you continue through this day it would be good to be more aware of your feelings. Try to recognize where the Lord seems to be leading you. As you move toward the end of the second week, it should begin to be clear to you what God is calling you to in this retreat. Can I begin to see if this is a school of prayer or a time of election? Can I see more clearly what his word to me is at this time? We will focus more on these questions tomorrow, but it would be good to begin to ask them now.

The Scripture for Today   As regards the scriptural content of our prayer, keep in mind the suggestion that we focus each day on the grace which we seek. As we said yesterday, the outline (see pages 173-175) is designed for a more complete 12-day retreat. But since most guided or directed retreats last eight days, I suggested that beginners take day four on the outline, while pray-ers who are more mature could take day seven. Similarly for today, those who are relative beginners could take five. The grace then would be to experience 1 Corinthians 2:10-16, and the theme Jesus' proclamation of the kingdom. In this case, you would use Matthew, chapters 5 to 7; or Mark, chapter 2 verse 1 to chapter 3 verse 12; or Luke, chapter 4 verses 14 to 30, and chapter 6 verses 20 to 49; or, finally, John, chapters 2 and 3. You continue, as a beginner, to search out the call of the king and the initial demands of his kingdom.

If your prayer life is more mature, you could use instead day eight on our outline, where the grace is to experience 2 Corinthians 5:16—6:10. As we saw, the difference is that days seven, eight and nine focus on the challenge of Jesus to Peter after he has already proclaimed Jesus to be the Messiah. At this time the first state of his formation has been completed and the challenge of a suffering Messiah is presented to him. For those who are more mature, the focus today would be on our response to Jesus' challenge. The passages to choose from are Matthew, chapters 15 and 16; or Mark, chapter 8 verse 11 to chapter 9 verse 1, and chapter 10 verses 17 to 27; or Luke, chapter 18 verse 9 to chapter 19 verse 10; or, finally, the great eucharistic discourse in St. John, chapter 6.

Let us recall again that, since our focus is on the grace, the scripture or the corresponding parts of the *Spiritual Exercises* or of some other retreat conference book are all but means to the grace that we seek. So use as much or as little as helps you to the grace. In fact, if your prayer is in the dry well phase, your input may be simply the Pauline passage given as the grace. For example, 2 Corinthians 5:16—6:10 might be enough for this whole day. Certainly, that has been my own experience. Since the dry well has set in very little input is necessary or even possible. It is now more a question of living the whole day in the spirit of the grace.

Even the dryness can have a different coloring from day to day. That may sound strange, but to those who have experienced it, I think it will be clear enough. And it suggests a general phenomenon which we can note now that we are well-settled into the retreat. There is a certain maturing in prayer that St. Ignatius would expect even within the retreat. For example, beginners will usually find that it is much easier to pray as the days go by, provided that they are faithful and generous. They may find that the prayer of the first day or two is a struggle with a thousand distractions, and then they may be surprised later how much easier it is to come to quiet. They may find it very heavy at the beginning to spend a whole hour at prayer; later they may be surprised how much easier it is to stay that long and even at times a little bit longer.

So, too, more mature people whose prayer is initially more reflective or affective may find the first day or two very consoling and then find themselves encountering sustained dryness. The Lord may, and often does, take the retreat as an ideal time to lead us to a deeper level of prayer. In that case, the retreat may not be a time of election, of any big decision, but rather a school of contemplation. In that case the election, the decision or choice that we make is simply to say "yes" to God drawing us deeper. He calls us to let go of the security of our insights or of our feelings of his presence, and to let him draw us to something new, to a more transforming and less consoling prayer — prayer that is more like surgery than like a birthday party. That in itself is abundant fruit for one retreat.

Whatever is happening, it is all part of the putting on of the Lord Jesus. Provided you are generous and sincere, you should have somewhere deep within you a strong sense that he is truly working his will. Even if it is deadly dry, somehow this is a dryness that is burning out of me everything that is not Christ. Painful as it may be, it is the only way to become more one with him. As he learned obedience through suffering, so too, perhaps, must I. Certainly *I* must! So whatever is happening, it is the Lord. What we need and desire most is the gift of discerning love. Then we can be happy with whatever he is doing, as long as it is the Lord.

> No one should fool himself. If anyone among you thinks that he is wise by this world's standards, he should become a fool in order to be truly wise. For what this world considers to be wisdom is nonsense in God's sight. . . . No one, then, should boast about what men can do. Actually everything belongs to you: Paul, Apollos, and Peter, this world, life and death, the present and the future — all these are yours, and you belong to Christ, and Christ belongs to God. You should think of us as Christ's servants, who have been put in charge of God's secret truths. The one thing required of such a servant is that he be faithful to his master (1 Cor 3:18—4:2).

DAY SIX:

Responding to the Lord's Word

The Lord's "One Word" and Holy Realism
We now come to day six of our eight-day retreat. We have been praying over the Lord's public life for several days, and day six would normally be the final day of this second week. At this point the "word" of the Lord to us in this retreat should be becoming fairly clear. You recall that I mentioned at the beginning that in a good vacation with the Lord he has just one message, one word, so to speak, for us. From his point of view the whole retreat is a unity, and usually it is about this time in the retreat that this word of the Lord becomes clear. To help to this clarity, it can be very fruitful now to review our journal and, by means of a prayer-repetition, to see whether there is a consistent pattern to our experience — whether the Lord's speaking to us has really focused

119

on one thing that would be his message to us at this point in our lives.

I think that basically there are three elements in the *Exercises* which are geared to producing a "holy realism" in the retreatant. The normal danger in any retreat is that we can forget the difference between the mountaintop and Jerusalem. While we are on retreat, while we are on the mountain, the experience of the transfiguration can be very real to us. But we know from past experience that we have to return from the mountain to Jerusalem. We also realize, if we have come to know ourselves at all, that it is very easy to lose the clarity of vision and the conviction which we had on the mountaintop at the time of the transfiguration. So, our holy realism involves seeing our retreat concretely in the context of our daily life, not seeing it as an escape, a time apart in the sense that is totally unrelated to our daily life, but as having to flow over to and to be lived out in all the ordinary days to come.

As I said, there are three means to this holy realism. The first is connected with our prayerful discovery of the Lord's one message to us. When his word to us is clear toward the end of the second week, it is helpful to take the time to formulate a prayer expressing what this word is, what the message of the Lord to us has been and what our response is. You know, perhaps, that the church blesses with a plenary indulgence the practice of saying a prayer for perseverance in the good resolutions of the retreat for 40 days following the retreat. While it is true that is some ways our past use of indulgences led to abuses and thus Pope Paul VI wisely eliminated many of them, I think that this particular one has a very sound psychology behind it. The prayer that we say for perseverance over the next 40 days is, as it were, a sacrament of our experience, a way of keeping it alive and real to us.

What I like to suggest to my retreatants is that they formulate their own prayer, rather than just saying one of the familiar prayers they know. Take the time today to formulate a brief prayer expressing in just one or two sentences what the Lord's word to you has been, and what your response to him is. You can then say that prayer daily, not just for 40 days but throughout the year until your next good retreat. Many retreatants have told me that this prayer was a very great help in keeping alive the vision and the spirit of the retreat once they returned to the pressures of daily life. I recommend that in the afternoon or evening of this day as the second week ends, you formulate a brief prayer which you can use as a sacrament of your experience with the Lord throughout the year to come.

The other means which St. Ignatius gives us to this holy realism for keeping our retreat down to earth are, first of all, the third and the fourth weeks, and second, the contemplation for attaining the love of God. The first of these means we will introduce on day seven. The third week is Calvary and the fourth is the resurrection. But, as we shall see, our contemplation of those mysteries has a very definite purpose for St. Ignatius. They are not just meditations on the paschal mystery but are ordered toward a very special type of confirmation, toward the realistic living of our retreat in the weeks and months and years ahead. Similarly, we will see that the famous contemplation for attaining love, with which the *Spiritual Exercises* end, is the third means that Ignatius gives us to ground a holy realism.

For the moment, though, let us notice that the need in a good retreat is for sobriety. I believe that those active in the Cursillo say that the most important time is the "fourth day," even though the actual Cursillo lasts only three days. The fourth day, as I understand it, is the rest of one's life. Similarly, the important fruits of a good retreat are harvested as we live it out. Sometimes directees tell me that they have found the retreat very fruitful, that it has been a great experience in their lives. I always reply that I am delighted to hear that, but that what will be more important and more meaningful is how they feel six months from now.

So we need to be sober. In connection with this, it is good to be very careful about making promises or plans of life in time of retreat. It is not that these are bad, but it is important that we be sure that what we are commiting ourselves to is coming from the Lord and not from us. We can make many promises when we are high, when we are emotionally charged up, which we won't be able to keep later. In fact, promises like that do more harm than good, because when we realize we failed to keep them, we end up becoming discouraged and frustrated. We may even give up the basically good life which we were living before the retreat. That is the point of Jesus' parable about the seed that fell on shallow ground: Because it had no roots, it sprang up very fast; but also because it had no roots, it died equally quickly.

The Challenge of Discerning Consolation

This brings us to another important topic: How do we determine what the Lord is asking of us? To answer that question, we must consider the rules for discernment for the second week, as they are called. These rules, in paragraphs number 328 to 336 of the *Spiritual Exercises*, are the rules for consolation. Recall that we said earlier that the rules of the first week deal almost entirely with desolation precisely because desolation is the devil's normal way of working on beginners. He seeks to convince us that the new venture is too difficult, that it's not human, that it's too costly, that we can't make it. But once we are committed, which is the situation of a retreatant moving through the second week, desolation won't be such an effective tool for the devil in working on us.

Here we come up against one of the great paradoxes of our lives, especially our lives as discerning persons. It is that, while desolation is very painful, it is quite easy to discern; whereas consolation is both pleasant and ambivalent. Desolation is never God's voice, as we said earlier. It cannot be God, and therefore the discernment of desolation is rather simple. Unfortunately, consolation is both more enjoyable and much more complex. What I mean is that, whereas desolation can never be from God, consolation, while it should be God's voice, may not be. Consolation then is more ambivalent. It can be from the Lord or it can be from the evil spirit. For many years that puzzled me, but I think I now understand. St. Ignatius tells us that, properly speaking, the voice of God is the voice of consolation, and the voice of the devil is the voice of desolation. With committed pray-ers this *should* always be the case. The problem is that, while God is truthfulness itself and therefore can never deceive us by imitating the voice of Satan, unfortunately Satan is the father of lies. He is not under any constraint to be consistent and truthful. For that reason, when he cannot affect us by desolation, he has no scruples about imitating the voice of God, trying to attack us and confuse us by false consolation.

This, I think, is the reason why consolation turns out to be much trickier, much more of a challenge to the pray-er and to the director. Fortunately, Ignatius gives us some very important guidelines for distinguishing between the consolations which are from God and those which are from the evil spirit. He tells us in the second rule of the second week, paragraph number 330, that God alone can give consolation to the soul without any previous cause. That kind of consolation, which we will have to explain, can only be from God. By contrast, in rule three, paragraph number 331, he talks about a consolation which has a preceding cause, which he says can come either from the good angel or from the evil spirit, although for quite different purposes.

The first thing we have to explain is the distinction between consolation with and without any preceding cause. In number 330 in explaining the phrase "without previous cause," Ignatius says that it is "without any preceding perception or knowledge of any subject by which a soul might be led to such a consolation through its own acts of intellect and will." So it seems that a preceding cause is some reflection in the understanding, some image in the imagination, some activity of the senses, which leads us to a sense of joy, peace or consolation. If there is any prior activity in the senses or the faculties, then the consolation has a preceding cause. If there is no such activity then the consolation is without preceding cause.

As may be obvious, the conclusion we can draw is that most of the consolations in our lives, especially for beginners, are *with* preceding cause. When we meditate on the scripture, that is a preceding cause. When we contemplate imaginatively, that is also a preceding cause. Similarly, when we think of our favorite hymn, when we recall God's blessings, when we think of a friend that we love, when we see a beautiful sunset — all of these activities are preceding causes in our senses and natural faculties which lead to consolation, to joy in the soul. In such cases, as we will see in a moment, the consolation may be from God or it may be from the evil spirit.

Before we turn to that more common situation, though, it is good to notice that if a consolation is really without any such cause, then we can be sure that it is from God. We can be sure that the inspiration to act arising in such a consolation is from him also. But what would such a consolation without preceding cause be like? I can think of two examples of consolation which would be without sensible cause. In the first case, there are preceding causes but they are such as to produce *desolation*. I am criticized; I am frustrated in my work; painful experiences come to mind which would normally lead me to desolation and perhaps do lead me to it. Then I come before the Lord, feeling very low and unable even to reflect or to relieve the desolation, and in that dark situation I suddenly find myself at peace. There is peace in the soul even though the senses are still disturbed. I have a strong sense that the Lord is saying to me. "You came here for me, so what others think does not matter." That, I think, would be one example of a consolation without cause, and therefore one that is surely from God. Similarly, I think the consolations of the dry well, of pray-ers whose prayer has moved into the dark night, are often without preceding causes in the senses. Indeed, the whole sensible and even the reflective, imaginative level seems to be totally blank. Sometimes such persons will tell me that they were very empty, or even very distracted, and yet somehow at a deeper level they were at peace.

Both of these, I believe, are examples of consolation without a preceding sensible cause. The only warning Ignatius gives us about them is in rule eight (#336). While he says they are surely from God, still we have to distinguish between the actual time of the consolation and what we might call the "afterglow." This calls our attention to a situation that can be dangerous, especially for beginners. My consolation, my experience of God may be quite genuine, and yet after the experience passes I can still be on a "high." At that time I may be inclined to start thinking of what return I shall make to the Lord for his great love. I can devise all sorts of promises and projects which are not really inspired by him. They are not part of the consolation experience itself but rather of what we called the afterglow, when we are still high from some previous, genuine experience of God. So Ignatius tells us that we should be cautious to distinguish between the actual consolation and the time following when our faculties are active and the evil spirit can come in. In that sense, the consolation without preceding cause also has to be discerned carefully.

Examining the Beginning, the Middle and the End   Similarly, where there is a preceding cause from the outset we have to be very careful. Here St. Ignatius tells us that the devil can come in as an angel of light. He devotes four rules (#331-4) to explaining consolation with preceding cause as against the two rules which treat of that without cause. This, I think, is because the consolations with preceding sensible cause are much more usual in our lives, especially for the types of persons for whom he originally wrote the *Exercises*. What he tells us, in essence, is that we can always recognize the devil's designs by observing carefully the whole course of our thoughts. That is, if the whole experience (beginning, middle and end, as he puts it) is good then we can trust that the inspiration is from God. But if, we might say, we see the tail of the snake anywhere, then we should mistrust the whole experience.

In the beginning: For example, when I am praying, am I in the right place at the right time for the right reason? If I am praying in order to impress others, if I have gone to prayer with my arms outspread before the altar quite aware of the impression of holiness this may create on those around me, then the consolations that follow, however real they may seem, should not be trusted. Or if I go to prayer when I should be doing something else, for example, when charity or obedience requires that I be working or studying and yet I am very much drawn to prayer, there again is the tail of the snake in the beginning.

No matter how beautiful the consolation may be, we should not trust it.

Ignatius' reference to the middle, I think, refers to the actual time of consolation itself. What am I moved to during the consolation? For example, if I find myself judging others as failing to measure up to my own holiness, my own closeness to God, of if I find myself resenting the fact that I did not have the opportunity to come so close to God in the past because others didn't form me right, or because they blocked my vocation — in short, if I find resentment or judgmentalism or self-righteousness entering into the "middle" of the consolation — there again is a clear sign of the tail of the snake.

Finally the end: If the consolation leads me, St. Ignatius says, to something evil, for example if it leads me to separate myself from obedience or to abandon a life commitment which was made validly and in good faith, this again is the tail of the snake. The situation is especially tricky if the enticement is not to something clearly evil, but rather to that which is good but less good than the alternative. Sometimes, a sister or a priest may say to me, "My relationship with X must be good, because since I have loved her (or him) I have prayed so much better." St. Ignatius is telling us that this "good" result is not necessarily a sign that the friendship is inspired by God. The devil is willing to be very very pious as long as he can end up where he wants to. Indeed, if he wants to seduce a pious person, he knows that he will *have* to be pious in order to ensnare him or her.

If the beginning and the middle and the end of the consolation are all good, then we can trust that it is from the Lord. But one common sign of the devil's working is that he makes us impatient with all this analysis. In our emotional high, our ecstasy with the Lord, it seems silly and irrelevant to stop and observe and evaluate. We feel that the experience has to be good. That kind of restlessness, that kind of unwillingness to exercise a healthy caution, is one of the surest signs of the devil's working on pious people. That is why the retreat situation, with its distancing and time for prayerful reflection, is an ideal occasion to discern the direction of our lives. As we "come aside and rest awhile," the devil's deceits become clear.

So much more could be said about these ambivalent experiences of consolation, but for the moment let us recall that the context of my remarks here is that love leads to action or commitment. Our experience of the Lord in the retreat calls for response. God's love is always active and dynamic, and the love he gives to us and draws out of us is also active and dynamic. Therefore, the exclamation of the psalmist in psalm 116 expresses beautifully the disposition of the true lover of God: "What return shall I make to the Lord for all that he has given to me?" The point of the preceding paragraphs is that, if there are signs that we are in desolation, then we should never trust the inspirations to act which come at that time.

Of equal importance, as we have just seen, is that if there are signs of false consolation, we should never trust the accompanying inspiration to act either. As I say, the devil is willing to sing Gregorian chant, he's even willing to be the soloist in the church choir, if only he can bring us to his own ends.

He is willing to foster a very strong sense of social justice in us if only he can end up separating us from the faith. He is also willing to foster in us a very great zeal for orthodox dogma and orthodox religion, for purity of faith, as long as he can lead us to intolerance and narrow-mindedness. So we have to be careful in trusting and acting upon our inspirations.

Caution, though, does not mean cynicism. The Lord does work. I have seen him work in virtually every one of the hundreds of retreatants whom I have directed over the past 20 years. And he works beautifully. The problem is that he is not the *only* one working. So, as we contemplate his life and as we are drawn to ask what return we can make to him, it is good that we desire to make a return. All that is necessary is a dose of *healthy* caution, in order that we not be led astray by the devil insinuating himself into our religious experience and turning it to evil. We see so many examples of that happening to good women and men in the history of the church that we should be humbly (but trustingly) aware of the fact that it could also happen to us.

The Prayer of Day Six   To turn now to the theme for our day: In keeping with our procedure on previous days, I would suggest that a relative beginner in prayer follow day six on the retreat outline (page 174). This means choosing one of the following: Matthew, chapters 9 and 10; or Mark, chapter 3:13 to 4:41 plus chapter 6:7-13; or Luke, chapter 5:1-11, chapter 6:12-16, chapter 9:1-27, and chapter 10:1-24; or finally, John, chapter 4 (the Samaritan woman). We mentioned earlier that it is good to stay with one of the gospels throughout, so continue today with whichever gospel you have been using thus far. As you continue, contemplate Jesus' mission, his sending out of disciples to propagate the kingdom which the king has already proclaimed. Today, too, he chooses disciples, men and women, whom he sends out to do the good work for him. Basically, that is the theme of day six, and this sending theme forms a beautiful background for our consideration of what the Lord's word or message to us is at this point in our lives. How concretely is he calling me to live his love and to share his life with others?

On the other hand, if you have a more mature experience of prayer and have been making retreats for several years, my suggestion for today is to concentrate on day nine, the Church: Glory and Suffering. You notice that days seven, eight and nine focus on the theme of challenge — the deeper challenge to commit our lives to the crusade of a suffering Messiah. That was what Peter found so difficult to accept. He could, after day six, accept Jesus as Messiah; but it staggered and horrified him to think that being Messiah meant being a suffering servant. To pursue this theme on day nine, you can choose one of the following: Matthew, chapters 17 and 18, as well as chapter 20:17-34; or Mark, chapter 9:2-13 and 30-50, and also chapter 10:32-45; or Luke, chapter 9:28-62 and chapter 17:20-37. Finally, if you have been praying with St. John, take chapter 9 and also chapter 12:12-36.

The challenge of Jesus to follow him, to take up our cross with him, calls for a response, and that response is to be lived out by us not only as individuals but as a community. The kingdom (the church) is the seed, the leaven, the yeast which is to leaven the whole mass of the world. Since our call is ecclesial and not merely individual, it might be good to say a few words here about the place of social justice in a good retreat. For many years the question has been asked whether and how the *Spiritual Exercises* can be used as a tool for social justice, which is one of the great concerns of our day. I myself have felt for a long time that the answer to the first question is "no," not because social justice is unimportant but because I don't think the *Exercises* can be *used* for anything. As St. Ignatius tells us (#15), in the *Spiritual Exercises* we have to be, above all and more than at any other time, totally open to whatever the Spirit wants to say to us as retreatants. We cannot, as it were, channel the grace of the retreat into a specific direction of our own choosing. We cannot try to harness the energy of the Spirit for a particular end, no matter how good or how urgent it may seem to us.

At times I am asked to give a retreat and am told that the whole group of retreatants will be superiors. I always say to the one inviting me, "If I am free I would be happy to accept such a retreat, but I will give the same retreat to superiors that I would give to anyone else." I don't think that we can, as it were, bind the Spirit by *obliging* him to speak to these people about their roles as superiors. Similarly, when one makes a retreat preparatory to ordination, I would not center the whole retreat on the topic of ordination, beautiful and central as that may be. What I would *expect* to happen is this: In the second week, when we come to the concrete question of our way of following Christ, the Spirit would have much to say to the ordinand about his ordination — or to the superior about the role of leadership and service. I would expect the Spirit to do that, but I would want to be very careful to keep out of the way and not in any way do his work for him or force his hand. Although it might be a bit unusual, it is quite conceivable that he might want to talk to this ordinand or that superior about something else. It would be dangerous if I prevented any retreatant from freely hearing that divine something else.

To come back, then, to the question of social justice, my own feeling is that one cannot possibly contemplate the gospel of Jesus without confronting this challenge. The concern which is so prominent today that evangelization and justice go hand in hand — the vision of social justice as an essential precondition and foundation of any genuine evangelization — is not new. It may be newly rediscovered by us, but it comes out of every part of Jesus' preaching in the gospel. So a retreatant who is truly open to the scripture and who is a daughter of her time, or a son of his time, will very likely see that dimension and in some important way be affected by it. But we don't want to bind the Spirit because *we* see the urgency today of this aspect of discipleship; we don't want to dictate to him what he must be saying to this person at this moment.

I can well imagine, for example, that if I had retreatants whose whole life had been given over to social service and to commitment to the poor, then a deepened social concern might not be the greatest need for them here and now. In fact, it could be dangerous if they focused their retreat, by their own choice, on that area. If you recall, when we spoke of the rules for desolation we said that the devil acts as a military commander (paragraph 327, rule 14), concentrating the energies of the retreatant on the walls of his or her fortress that are already strong. In this case that might be the wall of social concern. Suppose, for example, that someone has been totally and generously involved in work for justice while the wall that is weak is his or her own interior faith life. With such a person, the devil will be quite happy to devote the whole retreat to social concerns where the person is already strong if by doing so he can keep attention diverted from the area of interiority and faith where he or she is weak.

The evil spirit could even make a retreat like that focused on social justice quite consoling and "fruitful" if doing so served his own ends. This realization more than anything else makes painfully evident the importance of discernment in the lives of committed women and men. We are journeying through a minefield where the most attractive and safest-appearing places may be booby trapped! This is why Jesus repeatedly exhorts the disciples to vigilance and sensitivity to the "signs" of the times and seasons. But note, he urges us to be *careful*, not to be paralyzed by fear. The devil is indeed a treacherous adversary. Yet our faith and trust should be even stronger. The thing we believe, the thing we trust the Lord for, is that Satan could never *totally* deceive those who are open and discerning and those who are willing to receive direction. Somewhere in the process the tail of the snake will appear. For those who have the eyes to see and the openness to trust a co-discerner, that "tail" will be enough evidence to recognize that this is not the Lord.

To Be Sure and Strong   We return, then, to the retreat prayer which we mentioned at the begin-

ning of this day six. I suggested that we try to formulate in a prayer what the Lord's call to us is, and what
we are moved to respond to him. This is not an easy
thing to discern. But if you have been generous — if,
as you look back over these six days, you were
rooted and grounded in love on the first day so that
the love of God was very real to you, and if in the
first week that great grace of seeing yourself as he
sees you was given so that you were able to come
naked before the Lord in the second week — then it
should have been possible to really hear his word
discerningly and lovingly and peacefully, without any
gimmicks, without any manipulation and yet in a
spirit of deep and quiet love. And despite all the
snares which the evil spirit can try to set in your way,
we can with fair confidence say that you have seen
the Lord.

We will turn tomorrow to the third and fourth
weeks, and for the evening of day six I suggest that
we contemplate the theme of Gethsemane. As we
will see, the basic grace we seek in the third and
fourth weeks is the grace of confirmation. What I
mean by that in relation to what we have been saying
on this day is the following: Having heard the Lord's
word, having said our "yes" to it and having expressed it in our retreat prayer, we realize that we are
still human. You are still the person of whom Paul
speaks who sees the good and wants it and yet all
too often finds yourself doing something else. So we
will seek from the Lord, before you go back to the
challenges of everyday life, the grace to be confirmed not in the sense of making sure of his word,
but in the sense of being strengthened (the original
sacramental sense of confirmation).

We will explore the grace of confirmation tomorrow, and will see how Ignatius links it to our contemplation of Calvary and the risen life. I mention it
now to allay any doubts the evil spirit may suggest to
you as you come to the end of the second week. If it
is really Christ's word to which you say your "yes,"
then you can be sure of the grace and strength
needed to live that word in the days ahead. He is
faithful and true. He works in us the power to fulfill
his every inspiration. This is the ground of "holy realism."

> For I planned to visit you on my way to
> Macedonia and again on my way back. . . .
> In planning this, did I appear fickle? When
> I make my plans, do I make them from
> selfish motives, ready to say "Yes, yes"
> and "No, no" at the same time? As surely
> as God speaks the truth, my promise to
> you was not a "Yes" and a "No." For Jesus
> Christ, the Son of God, who was preached
> among you by Silas, Timothy and myself,
> is not one who is "Yes" and "No." On the
> contrary, he is God's "Yes"; for it is he who
> is the "Yes" to all of God's promises. That
> is why through Jesus Christ our "Amen"
> (our "Yes") is said to the glory of God (2
> Cor 1:16-20).

DAY SEVEN:

Loved Unto Death

The Grace of Confirmation   On this seventh day of our retreat, we come now to the time of confirmation. Recall briefly the dynamics of the *Spiritual Exercises*: The second week, the time of knowing and loving and following Christ, is really the heart of the whole experience. As we mentioned more than once, our self-knowledge in the first week and our knowledge of the Lord, of the way he desires to fill us and desires us to follow him, go hand in hand. I also suggested to you in discussing day six that it would be good to formulate a prayer expressing briefly what the Lord's word to you has been during these days of the second week, since it is the time of commitment, of decision.

Yet, when we have heard the Lord's word to us and have responded with our "yes," the retreat is not finished. Sometimes retreatants do feel that it would be good to return immediately to the apostolate. Since I have heard the Lord's word to me, why not get on with the living of it? It would be a mistake to think so, however. The third week, which is Calvary and to which we devote this seventh day, and the fourth week, which is the risen life and about which we will speak and pray tomorrow, are a very important part of the retreat. They have as their purpose confirmation, that is, to be confirmed or strengthened for our living of the word that the Lord has spoken to us.

The *Exercises* give us two means to thus strengthen ourselves for the living out in the days to come the vision we have had of the Lord during retreat. With that holy realism of which I spoke yesterday, we want our retreat to last. We want our vision of the Lord on the holy mountain to be for us, as the transfiguration experience was in the second epistle of Peter (1:16-18), something which is alive and active and effective long after the retreat is finished. I mentioned that your prayer for perseverance is one of the ways of accomplishing this permanence. For St. Ignatius, the primary way is our contemplation of the mysteries of this third week and the fourth week, Calvary and the resurrection.

In keeping with Ignatius' advice (#3), I would suggest that you remain with the second week a bit longer if you feel that the Lord's word to you is not yet clear. If you have not yet been able to say with certainty what his message in this retreat is, then it would be helpful and desirable to stay with the second week theme until you are satisfied that you have heard and responded to his word to you today. There will be new words, new calls in the future, of course, and for those there will be other retreats. But what we want to realize now is the grace of this present moment.

If you feel that it has been realized, then I would suggest that we now look to the third and fourth week for that confirmation which is so important. I like to explain the Ignatian dynamic of confirmation in this way: The topic of the third week as I mentioned is Calvary, and the topic of the fourth week is the risen life. However, in the retreat we don't just contemplate these as central mysteries of our faith. It is true that the paschal mystery is the heart of our faith, the core of the earliest preaching of the church and of the sermons of Peter in Acts, perhaps the most ancient part of the New Testament. Still, in the *Spiritual Exercises* our contemplation has a definite purpose and focus. In the second week our contemplation of the public life of Jesus had a specific finality, namely, to discover how we are called to *follow* him; the four great thematic meditations, plus our various discussions of discernment, helped us to see that purpose more clearly. So, too, in this final part of the retreat we contemplate Calvary and the risen life of Jesus with a definite purpose in mind — as we have said, to be "confirmed."

By confirmation here we do not mean making sure, as one might speak of confirming an appointment or a reservation. After the second week we should be sure of the Lord's call already. Rather, confirmation is to be understood here in the sense of the sacrament of confirmation: to be *strengthened* in a commitment made, to be able to live it fully and faithfully in the days and the years ahead. To be thus confirmed, to be strong, I think we need two things. We need, first of all, to know that we are loved. It is the knowledge that we are loved that makes us able to face all the difficulties of life. I recall a friend of mine once saying to me that the job he had, which he disliked and found very frustrating but could not reasonably leave at that time, had meaning for him only because of his wife and his children. He could survive it because he loved them and was working and earning for them, and he knew that he was loved by them. I think the person with the most menial work, a garbage collector perhaps, whose job doesn't have much status in society, can still be a happy and fulfilled man if he knows when he comes home at night that for his wife he is the important and best garbage collector in the world. What society thinks won't be so important if he knows that he is loved at home. From this perspective, Calvary is the supreme proof of God's love. You contemplate it in the retreat not so much to grieve that your sins have brought the Lord there, although that is certainly part of the story, but to realize that he has loved you even unto death.

Knowing we are loved is not enough, however, as we shall see tomorrow. We also have to know, if we are to be confident and strong, that the one who loves us is strong. That, of course, is the meaning of the resurrection: that the Lord not only loves us unto death, but he who loves us is stronger than death. If you have deep in your heart those two realizations — that the Lord loves you and that the one who loves you is stronger than death — then I think you can be confident in facing the future. And your resolutions will not be *ningaskugon*, as we say in the Philippines: They will not be like the field-grass fire, which flares up very intensely and burns out very quickly, because they will be rooted in a love that is strong and lasting and faithful.

The Prayer of the Third Week   With respect to the third week, which we contemplate today, seek to realize that the Lord suffered and died for you *personally*. It is surprising how many truly good people never come to realize that or to be able to believe it. Perhaps they know it in the head, but to realize it experientially and to be able to hear the Lord say it to them is a great grace. That is the grace you ask today: to know that Calvary was for you personally. To express it very concretely, you might put the question to the Lord: "If I were the only person in the world, would you still have done this?" We know by faith that his answer is "Yes," but we need to hear it, not in books or from the pulpit but in our own encounter with the Lord in love. We need to hear *him* say it to us.

In contemplating the third week, which is days 10 and 11 on our outline (page 175), we might again distinguish between beginners and more mature pray-ers. For beginners, I think it might be very helpful to take today the narrative of the events of Holy Week as given on the outline for days 10 and 11: from St. Matthew, chapter 21, verses 1 to 17, and chapters 24, 26 and 27; from St. Mark, chapter 11, verses 1 to 11, and chapters 14 and 15; from St. Luke, chapter 19, verses 28 to 38, and chapters 22 and 23; or, finally, from St. John, chapter 13, verses 1 to 20 (which is John's account of the Last Supper), chapter 17 (the priestly prayer of Jesus), and chapters 18 and 19, which recount the passion proper. As I say, for beginners who still need to grow into the reality of the events, it would be good to read over quietly the whole passion narrative of the gospel you have chosen, to note those parts which strike you especially, and then to spend the day digesting and living those parts more deeply. Continue asking the Lord for the grace to realize and to experience that this was for you personally.

For more mature pray-ers who are very familiar with the events of the passion — who have long contemplated them, who have wept, who have realized the Lord's love for them, and have perhaps come to experience that the Lord was thinking personally of them in his supreme gift of love — for such mature pray-ers it might be more helpful to focus today on one of the grace passages given for day 10 or day 11. For day 10 Hebrew 4:14 to 5:10 is the great passage in which the author of the letter to the Hebrews (perhaps St. Barnabas) reassures us that we do not have a high priest who is unacquainted with our own infirmity, but one who has been tempted in every way that we are. I find it beautiful at this point to enumerate my own temptations, and to ask the Lord one by one: "Is it really true that you were tested in this way, as scripture says?" Hebrews goes on to say that he learned obedience through suffering, that he was made perfect in this way. How strengthening it is to realize that the Lord of the kingdom has gone before us even in our temptations, that he will never ask of us anything that he has not faced himself.

You might also use the passage given as the grace for day 11, Philippians 2:1-11, which is one of the greatest hymns of the early church. Apparently, as the scripture scholars tell us, this passage in Philippians chapter 2 (along with Colossians 1:12-20 and Ephesians 1:3-14) is one of the early liturgical hymns which Paul incorporated into his letters. It was central to the theology of Martin Luther and also of St. Augustine, whom Luther loved. The hymn proper begins with the exhortation, "Let this mind be in you which was also in Christ Jesus: being in the form of God, he did not consider his divine equality something to be hoarded like a miser's money, but emptied himself, taking the form of a slave; and being found in human likeness, he became obedient even unto death." The emptying (or *kenosis*) of Jesus thus involves three stages. He emptied himself of his divinity to become human. But then he went even further and emptied himself unto death. And finally the third stage, "Yes, even to the death of the cross."

To appreciate the depth of this deepest emptying we have to realize that the crucifix, which has become an object of devotion and veneration for us, did not have the same beautiful connotation in the early church. If I am not mistaken, it took several centuries before the early Christians could find in the crucifix an object of devotion. As long as crucifixion was still practiced, it was the most ignominious form of death known — the death of the basest of criminals in the world of the early church. To venerate the cross would be like us hanging a guillotine or an electric chair over our altars; the grim connotations would be much stronger than any sense of devotion. Only when crucifixion ceased to be practiced could the crucifix become, as it is for us, an object of veneration. So when the author of this beautiful hymn says, "yes, even to the death of the cross," he sees here the ultimate in self-emptying.

There follow immediately those beautiful lines which link Calvary to the resurrection: "For which very reason God has greatly exalted him." Thus begins the ascent of the God-man who descended alone, we might say, and then returns to glory together with us. This is the pattern, too, of all the eucharistic prayers. The body of the prayer describes the Lord's descent into the fullness and the depths of our humanity, and then in the final acclamation we return with him to the Father, "through him and with him and in him." In Philippians 2 he is greatly exalted and given "the name," the Jewish title of divinity, and proclaimed "Lord," the Gentile title of divinity. So, for more mature pray-ers it might be helpful to presuppose the gospel events of this day and to live the day in the deeper meaning of the mystery, in the spirit of either the passage from Hebrews or this passage from Philippians 2.

Three Degrees of Humility   To help us "grasp the depth and breadth and height" of Jesus' love for us unto death, let us introduce at this point an exercise which St. Ignatius includes in the second week. Because our retreat is quite brief compared to the 30 days which he envisioned, I thought it might be a little too crowded if we had the kingdom, the two standards, the three classes of men and women *and* the three degrees of humility all as part of the second week. We might not have had time to digest all of them. But the three kinds or degrees of humility is generally considered to be the culmination of the apostolic mysticism of the whole *Spiritual Exer-*

cises — the high point of our retreat experience of God. And I think it can very appropriately be transferred to the third week, especially in a shorter retreat like this. For we can see the third kind of humility, the ideal that St. Ignatius presents to us, both as realized in Jesus on Calvary and, as Ignatius intended, as an ideal for our own lives. Seen in this way, it is the culmination, the goal of a life dedicated to following Christ perfectly.

So let us introduce the last of Ignatius' great thematic meditations now, and as we pray over it we can see it in both directions: as it is realized in Jesus himself and as the goal of our own lives. It is referred to on day eight of our outline (page 174), and in the *Spiritual Exercises* it is paragraphs number 165 to 168. Ignatius presents it as the background for our election or commitment to Jesus Christ. In number 165, he tells us that the first kind of humility "is necessary for salvation. It consists in this, that as far as possible I so subject and humble myself as to obey the law of God our Lord in all things, so that not even if I were made Lord of all creation, or to save my life here on earth, would I consent to violate a commandment, whether divine or human, that binds me under pain of mortal sin." Quite simply, then, the first degree is possessed when, no matter what is offered to me or what I could have at the cost of a single mortal sin, I would immediately say "No, it's not worth it. Nothing in the world is worth even a single mortal sin."

The second kind of humility, which Ignatius says is "more perfect than the first," involves the same attitude with regard to deliberate venial sin. That obviously is a rather high degree of perfection:

where I would not *deliberately* commit even a venial sin for anything in the world, no matter what I was offered. And it is significant that St. Ignatius introduces this second kind or degree of humility in a rather surprising way. He says, "I possess it if my attitude of mind is such that I neither desire nor am I inclined to have riches rather than poverty, to seek honor rather than dishonor, to desire a long life rather than a short life, provided only in either alternative I would promote equally the service of God our Lord and the salvation of my soul" (#166). I say this is a surprising introduction because it is not immediately evident (or, at least, was not evident to me in my early years) how this attitude of detachment is related to our rejection of all deliberate venial sin. But, after many years and much struggle, I now understand. The reason he puts it this way is that one could never possess this second degree, one could never have that sense of horror of venial sin, unless he or she was truly detached from things like honor or dishonor, long life and short life. The root of all deliberate venial sin, I think, is precisely our attachments. It is because we do desire one alternative more than another that we compromise in what we might call small ways, even though we don't reject God totally.

It is worth noticing here, in respect to both the first and the second kinds of humility, that for Ignatius humility is *truth*. In this he is very close to St. Teresa of Avila, who makes clear that to be humble is to live in the truth. It is not to deny my gifts or to put myself down, but to be so possessed of the truth of who God is and who I am that I cannot act falsely. If we see humility in that way, then Ignatius' various degrees make good sense. In the first degree I am so aware of the truth of who God is and who I am that I could never deliberate over mortal sin. To do so would make no sense in the light of my living in the truth of God's identity and my own. Similarly, the second degree or second kind of humility would be a much deeper awareness of the truth of who God is and who I am, of what it means that he is Lord and I am creature. Even deliberate venial sin would make no sense for someone with this deeper grasp of the truth. From that perspective, I think we can also see that the second degree is, as Ignatius says, "more perfect that the first." Indeed it is, as I indicated earlier, really perfection of a high order. I would say, in the light of the third kind of humility which Ignatius presents as *the* ideal, that the second degree is really the perfection of the old law, of the Old Testament — the perfection of the Mosaic covenant.

I say that because when Ignatius introduces the third kind of humility he says, "This is the most perfect kind of humility. It consists in this. If we suppose the first and the second kind attained" — so this kind comes only after we already possess the first and the second — "then whenever the praise and glory of the Divine Majesty would be equally served" — so there is no question of sin here, no question of even venial sin in my choices — in such a situation, where I move beyond the law and obligation, then "in order to imitate and be in reality more like Christ our Lord, I desire and choose poverty with Christ poor rather than riches; insults with Christ loaded with them rather then honors; I desire to be accounted as worthless and a fool for Christ, rather than to be esteemed as wise and prudent in this world. For in this way Christ was treated before me."

This third degree of humility is usually quite intimidating to retreatants. It seems to propose to us as an ideal that we should *choose* poverty, choose insults and humiliations and choose to be rejected and despised. Indeed, the third degree is often presented that way, but I think the real meaning is deeper. If I read correctly, the important words here are "with Christ," "for Christ," "like Christ." What matters is not so much the poverty and the humiliations and the humility, but rather the being *with Christ* in all of these things. If we can see it that way and be true to St. Ignatius, then I think it makes eminent sense to say that this is the most perfect kind of humility. If the second kind is the perfection of the law, then this third kind is the perfection of love. What I desire is to be wherever Christ is. Sin is no longer a central concern or the principal criterion; it is presupposed that I would now have a horror of sin. But I go beyond the law to love. And the best of my choices is precisely my love of the Lord and my desire to be with him wherever he is.

Could Ignatius have said, "to be rich with Christ rich, and honored with Christ honored"? Yes, I think he could, because if that is where Christ is then that also is where we desire to be. At times in his life, for example on Palm Sunday, he was honored, and many of his friends (like Zacchaeus and the family of Lazarus) were rich or at least "comfortable." I think the reason Ignatius does not focus on that aspect is because, in choosing to be rich with Christ rich, we could easily be deceiving ourselves. That is, we would not know whether our choice was really because of Christ or because of the fact that the riches and the honor are things we naturally desire. We could claim that it is to honor Christ that we want to have grand churches and magnificent vestments, that we priests claim positions of privilege and respect. But in such situations of honor and wealth, it is very difficult to really trust our apparent motivation, to be certain that this is really done or chosen for Christ and with Christ.

The time when we clearly discover the true basis of our choice is in poverty and humiliation and dishonor. If we, like Ruth in her love for Naomi (Ruth 1:16-17), still desire and need to be with him even in his poverty and rejection, then we can be quite sure that the basis of our choice is love. We no longer have reason to doubt our motives. Thus if we see this third kind of humility as the perfection of New Testament love, as contrasted with the perfection of law in the second kind, then the growth and progression which Ignatius envisions becomes clear. We can also see that the third degree is truly beautiful and not frightening, although it is indeed beyond our capacity to accomplish ourselves. We can choose to be men and women of the third class; we can choose the standard of Christ and his kingdom. But here, in this third kind of humility, we are confronted with something that is beyond our choice. Either it is true or it is not true that I love the Lord that much. I can desire it, but I cannot make it happen. To love that totally is his gift.

Thus it is significant that St. Ignatius says, in number 168, "If one desires to attain this third kind of humility, it will help very much to use the three colloquies" — a famous Ignatian device for solemn moments, where I go to our Lady and ask her what I seek, and then go with her to the Lord Jesus and ask him, and then with the two of them to the Father to ask him. Here he says, "If one desires to attain this third kind of humility, it will help very much to use the three colloquies . . . (to) beg our Lord to *deign to choose him* for this third kind of humility." There I think we see the key: We can only ask to be chosen; we cannot choose. It is the Lord who chooses us for this level of love "which is higher and better, that (the person) may the more imitate and serve Him, provided equal or greater praise and service be given to the Divine Majesty."

Such love is true humility, a sure and deep grasp of the truth, and it is really the culmination of the whole Ignatian apostolic spirituality and of all the graces of the *Spiritual Exercises.* It is pure gift; we can only beg to be chosen. I always tell retreatants, however, not to ask for it unless they really mean it. Because it is something which the Lord desires far more than we do. If we sincerely ask for it, he will surely give it. We can say, quite literally, that he has died to give it to us. That brings us back to our consideration of the third week. I mentioned earlier that we can fruitfully introduce these three kinds of humility here in the third week, especially in a short retreat, even though St. Ignatius places them in the second week before the election. This is so because we can see them from a double perspective. Jesus himself is the man of the third kind of humility: He loved the Father that way. That is, he desired to be with the Father wherever he was. "My food is to do the will of him who sent me." At the same time that we contemplate in him the perfection of the third degree on Calvary, we can also realize what it would mean for us to love him as he loved the Father. That, indeed, is the goal of our lives.

Gethsemane: The Heart of the Redemption

In confirmation of the above, and as a fitting conclusion to our discussion of this third week, let us consider the agony in the garden. Gethsemane, for example in Matthew 26:36-46, provides a profoundly revealing insight into Jesus' desire to be with the Father, and at the same time is very reassuring for us. If you are now ready to enter into the third week, and assuming that you are reading this chapter in the evening of the sixth day, I would suggest that you contemplate Gethsemane tonight. Ignatius stresses the value, the sacramentality of time and place; so the late evening might be a very good time to come to the garden with the Lord and with the three disciples who could not remain awake with him one hour.

I myself feel that the heart of our redemption is really here in the Garden of Olives. We tend to think of Calvary as the central act, and Gethsemane as a sort of preliminary to the crucifixion. But it has seemed to me, in my own prayer and reflection, that the decisive moment is actually in the garden. It is there that Jesus said his definitive "yes" to the Father. Gethsemane was a real struggle; Jesus even said, "If possible, let this chalice pass," which implies that humanly he thought it might still be possible. He hoped, at least, that it would be possible. However, he goes on to say, "Not my will, but yours be done." These are beautiful words of surrender. Yet, if we look at them closely and contemplate them, they seem to imply again that his human will and what he suspected the Father's will to be were different. His love for the Father, his desire to be where the Father was, was not a blind, mechanical, automatic thing. Even he felt revulsion in the face of rejection and death . . . and we should not expect to feel any differently. We should not feel guilty that we react as he did. We should not seek to be holier than Jesus himself!

At the same time we see the perfection of the third degree of humility here, not in Jesus enjoying the abasement of Calvary, but precisely in his ability to say to the Father, "Everything in me recoils at the prospect. Yet it is still more important to me to be wherever you are, beloved Father. If Calvary is where you are for me, even though humanly I would love to have it otherwise, let it be." This beautiful realization that we can be at peace with our humanity is for all of us tremendously supportive and encouraging, I think. We can know in a very concrete way that the Lord has been tempted in every way that we are, and yet he was able to say "yes" to the Father even in the face of his human revulsion.

So the third degree, as we said earlier and as we see revealed here in Gethsemane, is not a love for humiliations in themselves. We are not masochists. If we are normal, we have a real revulsion for that sort of thing. But the man or woman of the third degree of humility has a loving desire to be with the Lord wherever he is. If I may use a personal example, I recall when my father was dying in 1973. I was in Rochester for the last three weeks of his life. Each evening I would go home with my mother and the following morning we would return to the hospital. I remember that it struck me very much that, hard as it was for her to see him dying, she was quite restless in the morning until we got back to the hospital. She had to be there at precisely the moment that we were allowed to enter. She had no peace if we were late. Yet after he died, as I heard from her later, she didn't go near that hospital, and she didn't want to go near it for a least a year or two, even though her own doctor's office was in an annex of the same hospital. She didn't love the hospital, but she loved to be where my father was. In fact, if I can judge from her feelings after he was no longer there, she "hated" the hospital because of what it represented in terms of his suffering. Yet, when he was there, she *had* to be there.

If you can see the balance in that personal example, I think you have some idea of the meaning of the third degree and of the mystery of Gethsemane. You also realize why I would suggest that this is the heart of the redemption. I feel that when Jesus left the garden, he left with his crisis resolved. He had said "yes" to the Father, and that yes was forever. Calvary, I think, was simply the living out of the definitive yes which was given in the garden. It was terribly important, just as our living out of our vows, or our marriage commitment or our ordination, is also important. But if they really are what they should be, then the crucial yes has already been said.

Gethsemane takes flesh in the living out of Calvary. In our daily lives the retreat "yes" to God takes flesh in all the events which follow from that yes. But the crucial moment, the moment we might say toward which our whole retreat has been directed, is the saying of that yes — yes which, for us as for Jesus himself, will be strong enough and firm enough to sustain us in the challenge of living it out. It is encouraging to recall, though, that the ability to say "yes" in that way, to love the Lord to that degree, is not something we can achieve for or by ourselves. We can only "beg to be chosen," by the grace of the Lord and with the help of his holy mother, to love him so greatly. It is his gift. But, as I said earlier, I believe that it is a gift which he surely gives to those who sincerely desire it. He is dying — has died — to give it!

> Let us, then hold firmly to the faith we profess. For we have a great High Priest who has gone into the very presence of God — Jesus, the Son of God. Our High Priest is not one who cannot feel sympathy for our weaknesses. On the contrary, we have a High Priest who was tempted in every way that we are, but did not sin. . . . In his life on earth Jesus made his prayers and requests with loud cries and tears to God, who could save him from death. Because he was humble and devoted, God heard him. But even though he was God's Son, he learned through his sufferings to be obedient. When he was made perfect, he became the source of eternal salvation for all those who obey him (Heb 4:14-15; 5:7-9).

DAY EIGHT:

"Fear Not,
I Have Conquered the World"

The Prayer of the Fourth Week   We come now to the final day of our eight-day retreat, and to what is known as the fourth week of the *Spiritual Exercises* of St. Ignatius. To recall the whole flow of the experience: The integrating vision of knowledge of self in the first week and of knowledge of the Lord (putting on the Lord) in the second week led us to commitment, to a response of love to the love of the Lord revealed to us. And, as we saw in explaining day seven, the third and the fourth weeks (Calvary and the resurrection) have as their finality the grace of confirmation in the sense of strengthening. We noted that in order to be strong in living the word of the Lord to us at this moment in our lives, we need two things. First, we need to know that we are loved — and Calvary, as we have seen, is the supreme testi-

mony to the fact that the Lord has loved us personally, even unto death. But we also need to know that
the one who loves us is strong, that he has not only
loved us unto death, but that he has conquered
death. This, as I see it, is the way the fourth week fits
into the whole flow of the *Spiritual Exercises.* The resurrection is the proof, the ultimate proof, of the
power of this God of ours. So often, in the resurrection appearances in the various gospels, Jesus says
in effect, "Do not be afraid, for it is I. I have overcome the world, and so you have nothing to fear."

As we have seen, our retreat must be lived out
in the days ahead. The discernment which has
played such a central part in our conferences, and indeed is central to the *Spiritual Exercises* of Ignatius,
also has to be seen as a lived reality. Practicing this
art of discernment like any skill is of course awkward
in the beginning. The various rules and guidelines
which I treated so briefly, and which Ignatius
presents even more briefly, seem quite complex.
Sometimes people hearing of them for the first time
despair of ever being able to discern. The simple
process of loving the Lord seems so complicated
when we realize that his is only one of the voices
speaking, competing for our attention — and it is
true that we do have to contend with the world, the
flesh and the devil, all mimicking his voice. However,
I think we have to keep in mind that it is difficult to
learn any skill, any art. But with repeated practice
and perseverance we acquire an habitual facility. In
the case of discernment that facility is called discerning love.

We will say more about discerning love at the
end of this day. But let us consider first the theme of

the fourth week proper, the risen life of Jesus. On the outline (page 175) the fourth week is given as day 12. There I noted the appropriate passages from the various gospels. So whichever gospel you have been using, whichever evangelist has been your companion during these days of our vacation with the Lord, you could follow also on this final day and in this fourth week. For St. Matthew, the resurrection narrative is in chapter 28. In St. Mark's gospel, chapter 16 is appropriate, although Mark's final verses seem to be just a summary of the appearances in the other gospels. There is good reason for believing that Mark's original gospel may have ended with the empty tomb (or with some other conclusion which is now lost to us). In any event, since Mark's narrative is quite brief, one who is using Mark might supplement chapter 16 with 1 Corinthians 15:1-28. This is St. Paul's great profession of faith in the resurrection and his proclamation of what it means to us: that Jesus is the first fruits of those who have died; that what has happened in him is destined to happen in us too if we remain faithful until the end. In St. Luke's gospel the resurrection account is chapter 24; in St. John's it is chapter 20 and the appendix added after his death, chapter 21.

The Mystery of the Resurrection Narratives   It is helpful to note that the resurrection narratives have a rather peculiar, elusive character. To understand why, I like to take what we might call a concentric circles view of the gospels. The innermost circle of narrative would be the account of the passion of the Lord. That is what you find clearly affirmed (along with the fact of the resurrection) in the earliest sermons in Acts as the heart of the *kerygma* or the gospel proclamation. The next circle out from the center would be the public life of Jesus. An outermost circle would be the narratives of the resurrection. What I mean to imply by these three "circles" is this: The closer we are to the center, the closer the harmony you find in detail and in narrative among the four evangelists. The passion narratives come closest to forming a single story in all four gospels. There are indeed variations, but there seems to have been a concern from the very beginning to keep close to the facts. In the public life we also find substantial similarity among the various gospels, and yet we find much greater freedom in arranging and developing the events. As we noted earlier, wherever Mark and Luke have one blind man or one beggar, St. Matthew always has two. Incidents in Mark which have been taken over word for word by Matthew and Luke are often rearranged and placed at very different points in the narrative. So, in the public life, the second of the circles, while there is still considerable similarity among the four accounts, there is also much more variation.

The resurrection narratives would be the outermost circle in terms of historicity, once we recognize that the infancy narratives, the prologues to the gospels, vary entirely. St. Mark doesn't have any prologue; St. John's is the hymn of the Eternal Word; St. Matthew's focuses on the figure of Joseph; and St. Luke's on the figure of Mary. So these "overtures to the symphony" (which is what they are) have very little in common. They seem to be entirely unrelated to one another. Apart from the prologues, though, the part of the gospel in which the four evangelists show the greatest dissimilarity is the resurrection narratives.

It might be worth noting some of the striking peculiarities which we find there. For example, the order of the appearances. In St. Matthew, Jesus appears first to the two Marys in Jerusalem, and then he appears to the eleven in Galilee. In St. Luke's gospel, the two Marys don't see Jesus; they see only the angel. Then we have Luke's beautiful story of the two disciples on the road to Emmaus, in his account the first apparition of Jesus. This is followed by the story of the appearance to the eleven in Jerusalem (not in Galilee, as Matthew has it) that same Easter evening. So, whereas in Matthew the eleven see Jesus only in Galilee after the two Marys are told by Jesus to inform them to go there, in St. Luke's gospel they meet Jesus in Jerusalem on Easter night. In fact, as we shall see shortly, Jesus' ascension appears to take place that same Easter night according to St. Luke's gospel. In John, Jesus appears first to Magdalene, and not to the *two* Marys as in Matthew. After that, he appears to the *ten* in Jerusalem — in Jerusalem, as in St. Luke, but now only to ten of them. Thomas is only present at a third apparition eight days later. Finally, in the appendix to St. John's gospel, the disciples meet Jesus "later on" in Galilee on the shore of Lake Tiberias.

So we notice great variations in the resurrection accounts. In Matthew, Jesus appears to the eleven in Galilee; in Luke and John, he meets them in Jerusalem. In Luke, all eleven are present; in John, only ten are present and Thomas comes later. Luke seems to imply that Jesus ascended into heaven on

Easter night after the Jerusalem appearance, whereas in John and Matthew he remains among them for several days at least. St. Mark's gospel, which as we said seems to have lacked a resurrection narrative or to have had one that is now lost, has been completed in the canonical version with appearances to Magdalene, to two disciples on their way "to the country," probably Emmaus, and then to the eleven at the table, after which Mark recounts the ascension. So we find in Mark's summary account some echoes of Luke and some of John.

As you read the above, it may all be quite confusing — and that is precisely the point that we want to note! Whereas we get a clear sense of the narrative flow in the public life and in the passion, even the variations not confusing us that much, here in the resurrection surprisingly, considering the central importance of this event to the faith of the disciples, we cannot even be sure whether Jesus appeared in Jerusalem or in Galilee. Nor to whom he appeared first. It seems to be a very mysterious situation, and the disciples' memories of it seem to be remarkably vague.

The Jesus of History and the Christ of Faith   There is evidence, moreover, of real doubt about the identity of the risen Lord. The doubts are of two kinds: those concerning the testimony of others and those concerning the disciples own experience of him. The former are easier to understand. For example, St. Mark in 16:11 tells us that the disciples did not believe Magdalene's report, and in verse 14 that Jesus reproached them for their unbelief and their obstinacy in not believing the reports of "those who had seen him alive." Similarly, in chapter 24 of St. Luke, verse 11, we read that the disciples did not believe the women; and in John 20:24 that Thomas did not believe the other disciples. Here we are dealing with the disciples' refusal to believe the reports of others, which despite Jesus' reproach is understandable in such extraordinary circumstances.

Far more mysterious, at least to me, is the fact that we find in St. Luke and St. John a failure to recognize Jesus even when they themselves encounter him. For example, in Luke 24:16, speaking of the disciples on the road to Emmaus, St. Luke says "they saw him, but somehow did not recognize him," even as they walked along with him. And in verses 37 to 39 of that same chapter 24, when Jesus appears to the eleven, they felt that they saw a ghost. He has to reassure them by saying, "It is really I." And a few verses later (24:41), St. Luke has one of my favorite lines in the whole of scripture: He says that the disciples "disbelieved for sheer joy" — a mysterious and wonderful kind of disbelief! They were so happy that they could not believe that this was really happening to them.

In St. John, 20:15, Magdalene does not recognize him. She thinks he is the gardener. And in verses 20 and 27 of the same chapter, the ten, and then Thomas, only believe that it is really he, only recognize him, when he shows them his hands and his side. There is another extraordinary and beautiful line in chapter 21:12 of St. John, when they are at the seashore for the breakfast that Jesus prepares for them by the lake of Tiberias. We read that none of them dared to ask him, "Who are you?" for "they knew quite well it was the Lord." A mysterious saying indeed! It is hard to imagine when we would say, "I did not dare to ask who that person was, for I knew quite well it was my friend Joe." I suppose we would only speak that way if for some reason we knew it *must* be Joe, yet somehow couldn't be sure or had reason to doubt.

We might say that the astonishment occasioned by the return of someone from the dead could explain this, but I think there is even more to it than that. We are dealing here with a Lord who is a "new creation." He is the same person, and yet he is not. It is here I see the relevance to our prayer of the whole mysterious aura of the resurrection narratives. Oscar Cullman, I believe, made a distinction between the Jesus of history and the Christ of faith. The disciples walking the roads of Galilee and of Judea during the public life saw the Jesus of history; they did not see the Christ of faith, the risen Lord who is experienced in quite a different way. The distinction is valid and quite helpful, provided we don't separate the Jesus of history radically and totally from the Christ of faith. They are the same person, but still Cullman makes a good point. Sometimes we say, "If only I had lived in the time of Jesus, how easy it would have been to believe." Yet all of the passages we have just cited make clear that is not true. It would have been just as difficult and perhaps even harder to believe in him as Lord if we had seen him as human, seen him weary from walking the shores of Galilee. Our *faith* is in the risen Lord made manifest, not only in the Jesus of history. Many people saw Jesus but did not see the Lord in him.

This helps to explain something which has puzzled me over the years: Oftentimes our prayer on the risen life of Jesus, in what St. Ignatius calls the fourth week, is more difficult and more intangible than in the preceding weeks. It is frequently quite hard to have the same experience of imaginative Ignatian contemplation when we come to the resurrection. There is a certain quicksilver quality about it, like the silver dollars in the lake which we used to grasp for when we were children swimming. Every time I tried to get them in my hand under the water they seemed to disappear. There is something similar about our prayer experience of the risen Lord. But if we realize that it is no longer simply the Jesus of Nazareth whom we contemplate, but a Lord whom some saw and some did not in the resurrection, whom some recognized and some did not — that it is the Christ of faith whom we contemplate — we can make more sense out of our experience. The Lord who comes to reassure us now is the Lord of glory, always with us until the end of the world, yet in some sense absent, in some sense out of our reach. That is why the New Testament, although it recounts his coming, yet ends with that beautiful cry, "Come, Lord Jesus!" He has already come, and still we live in a time of longing for his coming.

Living the Risen Life   Significantly, the place where the risen life takes flesh is in the Acts of the Apostles, that is, in the life of the early church, in the concrete and tangible experience of the first believers. I would suggest that we could continue our contemplation of the risen life either during this day or in the days that follow the retreat by praying over the first three chapters of Acts.

In Acts, chapter 1, we have what we might now call the "second" ascension of Jesus. As I indicated earlier, St. Luke seems to imply, as perhaps so too does Mark, that Jesus ascended on Easter Sunday. And in John 20:17 Jesus says to Magdalene, "Do not cling to me Mary, because I still must ascend to my Father; and you must go and tell the brethren" what you have seen. He seems to be referring to an immediate ascension. It is as if he had appeared to her on his way from the grave to the throne of God, out of due time, precisely because of her desperation. This beautiful Magdalene scene seems to imply that he interrupts his return to the Father for her sake, that his own resurrection is still incomplete when he takes time out to console and strengthen her. And Magdalene, I suspect, symbolizes all of us who love him in our weakness. In any event, if there are two ascensions as scripture seems to imply, we could say that this ascension on Easter Sunday is the culmination of Jesus' own mission. It is his return to the Father, his laying the world at the Father's feet and saying, "Father, I have done what you have asked me to do," and his being made perfect because of his obedience (cf. Heb 5:8-9)

By contrast, the ascension 40 days later in Acts 1 is the beginning of the "absence of Jesus" from our world, as the early church Fathers described the present age. It is the time when Jesus hands the world and his mission over to the Holy Spirit. If we live in the age of the absence of Christ, it is also the age of the Spirit of God. Let us contemplate the ascension as the beginning of this new age. And let us note, for our own encouragement, that right up until the end the disciples still did not understand Jesus.

Their very last words to him were, "Lord, are you finally going to lead the revolution?" Which means that even then, they *still* don't understand what his mission is all about! And he, very touchingly and, we might say, very humanly seems to give up hope of making it clear. He abandons the fight and tells them, "The Holy Spirit will explain it all to you." We might say he passes the buck to the Holy Spirit, in the face of their slowness and stupidity. How like us they were!

In chapter 2 of Acts we have the beautiful and momentous story of Pentecost, when Peter who was so timid becomes the Rock filled with the Spirit. In the beginning of chapter 3 of Acts , verses 1 to 10, is one of my favorite incidents in the whole of scripture. Peter and John encounter a cripple at the Beautiful Gate of the temple. Peter says to him, "Gold and silver I have none; but what I have I give to you. In the name of Jesus of Nazareth, arise and walk." It has struck me in recent years that there is a deep connection between the fact that Peter had no gold or silver and the fact that he could make the man walk. It is precisely because his pockets are empty that the power of the Lord dwells in him. That reflection forms a fitting climax to the whole experience of your vacation with the Lord. To the extent that your retreat has been truly fruitful, you too have emptied your pockets of whatever might be the gold and silver in your life in order that the power of Jesus may also dwell in you as you go out to meet the beggars by the beautiful gates of our world.

The Contemplation for Attaining Love   St. Ignatius suggests a concluding exercise, which comes after the fourth week in the text of the *Spiritual Exercises* (#230-237). He calls it a "contemplation to attain the love of God." I think this provides the final note of holy realism in the *Exercises,* and also the culminating fruit of the whole experience of a good retreat. You might ask: "Why only now do I seek to 'attain' the love of God? On the very first day of the retreat I contemplated God's gifts and sought to experience his love." What we seek to realize now, though, is that this is not only love received, but love given. Not only the love of God for you (and in that sense you do return to where you started), but also your response of love for God, which is equally his gift! St. John of the Cross says, "Where there is no love put love, and then you will find love." He seems to be speaking here of our love for the brethren. But I find his words most appropriate when I address them to the Lord himself. When he looks at me and finds very little love in me, I can with all justice and propriety say to him, "Where there is no love in me, you, Lord, put love, and then you will find love."

St. Ignatius gives two prenotes to this contemplation to attain the love of God. The first, which is typical of him, is that love should manifest itself in *deeds* rather than merely in words. Talk is cheap, and emotion too is cheap unless it leads to good works. The second prenote, which is deeper and more mysterious, is that love consists in a mutual sharing of goods, so that the lover gives to and shares with the beloved whatever the lover has or possesses, whatever he or she is able to give. So, too, does the beloved share with the lover. Love is reciprocal. It is what St. Thomas Aquinas called the love of friendship or *amor benevolentiae.* This highest form of love is a mutual "love of benevolence," each desiring primarily the good of the other. It is thus that God shares all he has with us, and we in turn are asked to share all we have with him.

You can read over the four points that Ignatius gives in this contemplation. Basically he suggests that you ponder, first, all that the Lord has given you of what he possesses, and that he even desires to give himself, insofar as you can receive him. Then ask, "What return shall I make to the Lord?" What can I give to him of my possessions and myself? This is where we find the beautiful prayer of Ignatius, "Take, O Lord, and receive all my liberty, my memory, my understanding, my will." The second point is that God not only gives everything, but he *dwells* in his gifts — in all his creatures and in me. What about myself? Do I dwell in the gifts I give? What would that mean? Thirdly, know that God not only gives and dwells in his gifts, but he is *always at work* in them. He is a God who is continually creating — not the watchmaker God of LaPlace who sets his creation in motion and then leaves it to its own resources. Jesus says in John's gospel (5:17), "The Father works even until now and so must I." Again, what of us? Are we forever responsible for the rose we have tamed? Are our gifts given once and for all, or are we always working in them by the power of God in us?

The fourth and final point of Ignatius is quite mysterious, or at least it was so to me for some years. St. Ignatius says, "This is to consider all blessings and gifts as descending from above." Thus, my limited power comes from the supreme and infinite power above, and so too does justice, goodness, mercy, etc., "descend from above as the rays of light descend from the sun, and as the waters flow from their fountain." We have here, it seems, the principle by which I can give and dwell in and work in my gifts, because it is only by the power of God in me that I so act. It is because my being and my living and my working are a participation in God's, just as the rays participate in the sun's brightness, that I can even begin to hope to give to God as he gives to me.

I think that there may also be a deeper meaning here, one that has come to me in recent years as I thought about this fourth point of Ignatius' contemplation to attain the love of God. What he says took on more meaning for me in the light of something St. Teresa of Avila has to say in the later mansions of the *Interior Castle.* In the fifth, sixth and seventh mansions, she speaks of a number of supernatural graces which God can give to the soul, and at one point she mentions that none of these unusual gifts (ecstasy, visions, voices and so on) is necessary for holiness. She feels that all of them can help, but none of them is essential. As she says, the only grace which is really crucial to holiness is the union of *wills*, of our will with God's. But in speaking of the different unusual graces which she experienced, she mentions only one which we should ask for and desire (*Interior Castle,* VI mansions, chapter 10). All the others are best left to the Lord and we should not seek them or consider them essential. The one exception is an experience in her own life where she was given the grace, the supernatural grace, to *see all things in God* — even her own sinfulness. That is the one special supernatural gift which we should seek, for which we should ask. Why? Because, she says, if we could only see everything existing *in God*, even our own sins, she can't imagine that we would ever sin again!

I see this Teresian grace as connected with and illuminating the fourth point of Ignatius' contemplation for attaining love in this sense: The rays flow from the sun and participate in the sun's nature; the water flows from the spring and is of the same nature as the spring itself. If we see the water in the spring, if we see the rays in the sun, perhaps we are moving to a much deeper level of contemplation. Not only do we see God in all things — which perhaps could summarize the first three points of the contemplation: to see God creating and dwelling and working in all things — but in this fourth point, in the light of what St. Teresa says, we can say that the movement is reversed and we are called to see all things in God. Seeing God in all things can ultimately lead us to see all things, including ourselves and even our own sinfulness, in God.

For St. Ignatius this contemplation, which comes after the fourth week, seems to be a transitional prayer. You may not have time to do it in this single day when you also contemplate the resurrection, but it might be very fruitful to use it in the days following the retreat. That is, it might be helpful to make the contemplation the subject of your prayer after you leave the retreat as you move back into daily life.

An End and a Beginning   It is also helpful, at the end of a good retreat, to look back to the first day, the first night. I suggested then that you begin your retreat by contemplating the incident in chapter 8 of Acts, where we discover in Philip and the eunuch the ideal dispositions for a good retreat. I suggested at that time that you begin your journal by jotting down all of your hopes and your fears as you started this vacation with the Lord. As you come to the end tomorrow evening, it might be very fruitful to look back to that first evening and to see how your hopes and your fears look to you now. Have the hopes been realized? Has the Lord surprised you? How about the fears? Have they turned out to be justified? Or has the Lord, perhaps, surprised you there also? It can be fruitful to realize how different things appear to us now from the way they appeared at the beginning.

This realization can also provide encouragement for the future. Like Peter and James and John at the transfiguration, we are called to return to Jerusalem. Like Magdalene, when she encountered the Lord in chapter 20 of St. John, we cannot cling to him. The point is that she does not *need* to cling to him. He cannot be lost again. He is risen, he has overcome the world; she now has nothing to fear. So she too must return to the brethren, to the city, to the heart of Jerusalem, to her daily life — not regretfully, but joyfully, realizing that everything that she has received from the Lord is given to her for others. Her return to the world of her ordinary human experience is not a loss, but is the necessary fruit of her "vacation with the Lord." She can only keep the Lord she has found by giving him away. The same thing is true for us.

To return now to the point we mentioned at the beginning of this day, we have spoken throughout the retreat of discernment. Indeed, the longer I make and give retreats, the more deeply convinced I am that the art of discerning is the very heart of the *Spiritual Exercises* and the essential link between prayer and life. Discernment is where prayer meets action. In this connection, it is helpful to notice that the discerning dimension of our retreat, while it may have involved confronting a particular decision which we had to make or a particular election, actually has a deeper meaning than that. It is not *primarily* to make some specific decision that we come to retreat, but rather to become discerning persons — to acquire that habit of discerning love which is the mark of the mature apostle, the mature lover of the Lord.

As I said earlier, discernment can seem complicated and awkward when we are still learning the art, but as we live long in love it becomes second nature to us. It is a question of reading the face of God, of being able to see there what pleases him. It is sensing in events the presence of the good spirit and also, of course, the presence of the evil spirit, and of being able to tell the difference with the facility which is born only of long familiarity with both of them. That is the heart of the work of a spiritual director: to be a co-discerner, to bring that sensitivity to bear on the lives of others. It should be the great grace of a good retreat, and even more so of many good retreats made over many years. Because of our long living with the Lord, both in the marketplace of our day-by-day activity and in these special times when we come aside and rest awhile with him, we too should become truly discerning people.

It is this sensitivity which makes it possible for us to be women and men who do God's work rather than merely working for God. As all of our life becomes prayer, everything we do is marked by that "love by connaturality" which comes from a long life lived intimately with someone, learning to love and to think the beloved's thoughts just as Jesus did with the Father. It is to become one with him as he himself was with the Father, whom he loved above all things. If our vacation with the Lord has helped us to grow toward that goal, then it has been a truly fruitful time. We are ready to return to Jerusalem, with eyes better able to see him in all things and all things in him. And we will be much better instruments of his work in our world.

> "I do not ask you take them out of the world, but to keep them safe from the Evil One. Just as I do not belong to the world, so too they do not belong to the world. Dedicate them to yourself, Father, by means of the truth; your word is truth. I sent them into the world, just as you sent me into the world. And for their sake I dedicate myself to you, in order that they, too, may be truly dedicated to you. I pray not only for them but for those who believe in me because of their message. I pray that they may all be one, Father, . . . so that the world will believe that you sent me" (Jn 17:15-21).

RETREAT OUTLINE

This outline is structured for a 12-day retreat following the pattern of St. Ignatius' "weeks." Explanations are given to adapt these instructions to an eight-day retreat.

The suggested readings are from the Bible and St. Ignatius' *Spiritual Exercises.* Throughout the retreat, focus on the grace of the day. Use as much or as little of the suggested readings as is helpful to realize the grace sought.

INTRODUCTORY MEDITATION

Acts 8:26-40. Enumerating all my hopes and fears for this retreat and placing them in the Lord's hands.

PRINCIPLE AND FOUNDATION

Spiritual Exercises, paragraphs 1-23

Day 1: The grace to experience God's personal love and call as the foundation of my life (Eph 3:17-19).

Isaiah 43:1-7

Psalms 23, 27, 42, 103-105, 139

John 1:1-18

—or review God's blessings through my whole life

THE FIRST WEEK

Spiritual Exercises, paragraphs 45-90

Days 2-3: The grace to see and experience myself as God sees me (Rom 2:1-6).

Job 38-42

1 John 1-5

Romans 1-2, 5, 7-8

—or profile myself as I think God sees me and listen to him (with the help of the scripture above) confirm or correct my profile

THE SECOND WEEK: The grace to put on the Lord Jesus; to live "no longer I but Christ in me" (Gal 2:20).

Spiritual Exercises, paragraphs 91-189

Note: In an eight-day retreat beginners could focus on

Days 4, 5 and 6 while more mature pray-ers could pass over those days and move to Days 7, 8 and 9. The retreatant should choose one gospel to remain with for the rest of the retreat.

Day 4: The grace to experience Ephesians 5:6-14.

The King Appears

Spiritual Exercises, paragraphs 91-99, 127-131

Matthew 3-4	Luke 3:1—4:13
Mark 1	John 1:19-51

Day 5: The grace to experience 1 Corinthians 2:10-16.

The Kingdom Proclaimed and Discerned

Spiritual Exercises, paragraphs 136-148—The Two Standards

Matthew 5-7	Luke 4:14-30; 6:20-49
Mark 2:1—3:12	John 2-3

Day 6: The grace to experience 1 Corinthians 3:18—4:5.

The Mission

Spiritual Exercises, paragraphs 149-157—The Three Classes of Persons

Matthew 9-10	Luke 5:1-11; 6:12-16; 9:1-27; 10:1-24
Mark 3:13—4:41; 6:7-13	John 4

Day 7: The grace to experience 2 Corinthians 1:15-22.

The Challenge of Jesus

Spiritual Exercises, paragraphs 328-336—Discernment

Matthew 11-12	Luke 11:37—12:59
Mark 6:30—7:23	John 5, 7-8

Day 8: The grace to experience 2 Corinthians 5:16—6:10.

The Response to Jesus' Challenge

Spiritual Exercises, paragraphs 165-174—The Three Kinds of Humility and Election

Matthew 15-16	Luke 18:9—19:10

Mark 8:11—9:1;   John 6
10:17-27

Day 9: The grace to experience 2 Corinthians 4:7-18.

The Church: Glory and Suffering

Spiritual Exercises, paragraphs 175-189

Matthew 17-18;   Luke 9:28-62; 17:20-37
20:17-34   John 9; 12:12-36
Mark 9:2-13, 30-50;
10:32-45

THE THIRD WEEK

Spiritual Exercises, paragraphs 190-217

Note: In an eight-day retreat, combine the material given
in Days 10 and 11 for Day 7.

Day 10: The grace to experience Hebrews 4:14—5:10.

Jesus lives his teaching unto the end.

Matthew 21:1-17; 24;   Luke 19:28-38; 22; 23
26; 27   John 13:1-20; 17; 18; 19
Mark 11:1-11; 14; 15

Day 11: The grace to experience Philippians 2:1-11

Matthew 26:36—27:66   Luke 22:39—23:56
Mark 14:32—15:47   John 18-19

THE FOURTH WEEK

Spiritual Exercises, paragraphs 218-260

Day 12: The grace to experience Colossians 1:15-23.

Fear not, for I am with you always!

Matthew 28   Luke 24
Mark 16:1-20 and   John 20-21
1 Corinthians 15:1-28

CONCLUSION

The Contemplation for Confirming Love, *Spiritual Exercises,*
paragraphs 230-237

John 13:31—15-27